COLLI

EDINBURGH
STREETFINDER
COLOUR ATLAS

CONTENTS

HarperCollins*Publishers*

Legend / Légende / Zeichenerklärung

main through road
axe principal
Durchgangsstraße

dual carriageway
chaussées séparées
Straße mit getrennten Fahrbahnen

main link road
axe secondaire
Verbindungsstraße

other roads
autres rues
sonstige Straßen

lane, drive
petite rue, allée
Gasse, Einfahrt

walkway
passage
Fußgängerweg

path
sentier
Pfad

shopping centre
centre commerçant
Einkaufszentrum

ℓ **tourist information centre**
syndicat d'initiative
Informationsbüro

P **car park**
parking / Parkplatz

T **taxi rank**
station de taxi / Taxistand

♦♦ **toilets**
toilettes / Toiletten

• **post office**
bureau de poste / Postamt

▲ George **principal hotel**
hôtel important / führendes Hotel

CH **consulate**
consulat / Konsulat

public building
bâtiment public / öffentliches Gebäude

+ **church**
église / Kirche

▮ **tower block**
immeuble élevé / Hochhaus

★ King's **theatre**
théâtre / Theater

★ Cannon **cinema**
cinéma / Kino

★ ★ Usher Hall **public hall**
salle de réunion / Veranstaltungshalle

○ ○ Huntly Ho. Mus. **museum or gallery**
musée ou galerie d'art / Museum

★ **library**
bibliothèque / Bibliothek

△ **primary school**
école primaire / Grundschule

▲ **secondary school**
école secondaire / Höhere Schule

⊞ **hospital**
hôpital / Krankenhaus

Ⓟ **police station**
poste de police / Polizeiwache

Ⓕ **fire station**
pompiers / Feuerwache

railways
lignes ferroviaires
Eisenbahnlinien

⇌ **main station**
gare principale
Hauptbahnhof

⊕ **airport coach terminal**
aérogare
Abfahrt zum Flughafen

bus route
ligne d'autobus
Omnibusroute

⑤ **bus terminus** / *terminus d'autobus*
Omnibusendhaltestelle L.R.T. / E.Sc.

→ **one-way street**
sens unique / Einbahnstraße

traffic lights
feu de signalisation / Verkehrsampel

dense built-up area
noyau urbain
dicht bebautes Gebiet

open residential area
zone résidentielle
dünn bebaute Wohnfläche

industrial land
terrain industriel
Industriegelände

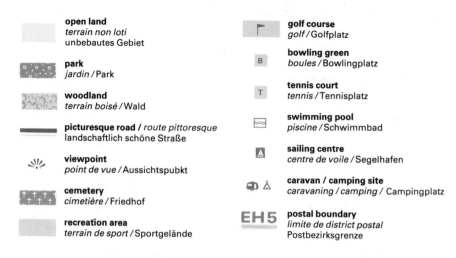

open land
terrain non loti
unbebautes Gebiet

park
jardin / Park

woodland
terrain boisé / Wald

picturesque road / *route pittoresque*
landschaftlich schöne Straße

viewpoint
point de vue / Aussichtspubkt

cemetery
cimetière / Friedhof

recreation area
terrain de sport / Sportgelände

golf course
golf / Golfplatz

bowling green
boules / Bowlingplatz

tennis court
tennis / Tennisplatz

swimming pool
piscine / Schwimmbad

sailing centre
centre de voile / Segelhafen

caravan / camping site
caravaning / camping / Campingplatz

postal boundary
limite de district postal
Postbezirksgrenze

Scale of main map pages - 1:15 000 (4.2 inches to 1 mile)

0   0.5   1   1.5 km

0   ¼   ½   ¾   mile

Consulates

(AUS) Australia	12	O19	
(A) Austria	18	J17	
(BD) Bangladesh	39	H12	
(B) Belgium	6	L16	
(CDN) Canada	6	L16	
(DK) Denmark	7	N17	
(F) France	6	L16	
(D) Germany	19	K16	
(GR) Greece	6	L16	
(IS) Iceland	12	N18	

(I) Italy	6	L16	
(J) Japan	6	L16	
(LV) Latvia	15	D18	
(MW) Malawi	11	M19	
(M) Malta	33	P14	
(MC) Monaco	6	L16	
(NL) Netherlands	6	M17	
(N) Norway	6	M16	
(RP) Philippines	6	L17	
(PL) Poland	11	L18	

(P) Portugal	12	O19	
(RO) Romania	6	L17	
(RUS) Russian Federation	6	L16	
(E) Spain	6	L17	
(S) Sweden	12	O19	
(CH) Switzerland	6	M17	
(UKR) Ukraine	7	N17	
(USA) United States of America	7	N17	

Collins
An Imprint of HarperCollins*Publishers*
77-85 Fulham Palace Road, Hammersmith, London W6 8JB

Copyright © Collins 1998

Based upon the Ordnance Survey mapping with the permission of the Controller of Her Majesty's Stationery Office.

© Crown copyright 399302.

The contents of this publication are believed correct at the time of printing. Nevertheless the publisher can accept no responsibility for errors or omissions, changes in the detail given or for any expense or loss thereby caused.

Printed in Italy

ISBN 0 00 448713 3

LNR   LI9658

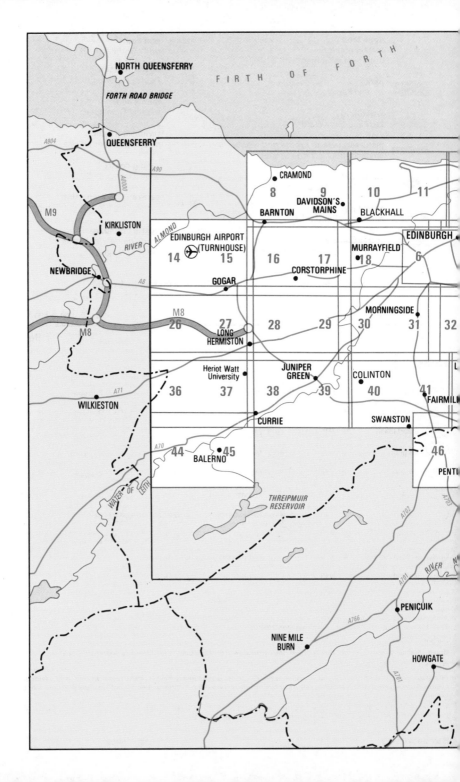

NORTH QUEENSFERRY

FIRTH OF FORTH

FORTH ROAD BRIDGE

A904

QUEENSFERRY

A90

A8000

M9

KIRKLISTON

ALMOND

RIVER

CRAMOND

8   9   10   11

DAVIDSON'S
MAINS

BARNTON   BLACKHALL

EDINBURGH

EDINBURGH AIRPORT
(TURNHOUSE)

MURRAYFIELD

14   15   16   17   18   6

CORSTORPHINE

NEWBRIDGE

A8

GOGAR

M8   MORNINGSIDE

M8   26   27   28   29   30   31   32

LONG
HERMISTON

A71   Heriot Watt
University   JUNIPER
GREEN   COLINTON

WILKIESTON   36   37   38   39   40   41

FAIRMIL

CURRIE   SWANSTON

A70   44   45   46

BALERNO   PENTI

THREIPMUIR
RESERVOIR

A702   A70

WATER OF LEITH

A101   RIVER   N

PENICUIK

A766

NINE MILE
BURN

HOWGATE

A701

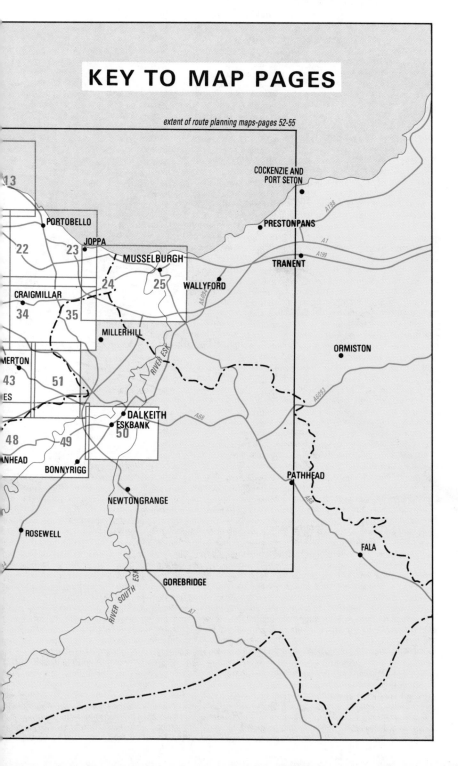

KEY TO MAP PAGES

extent of route planning maps-pages 52-55

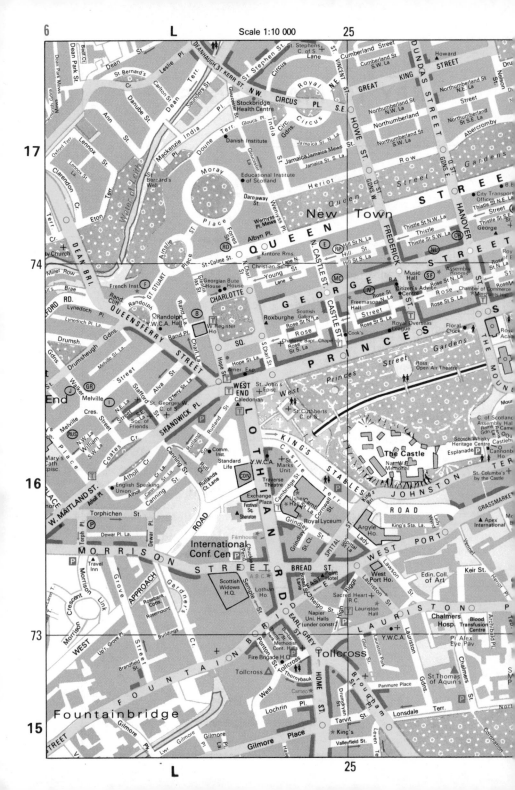

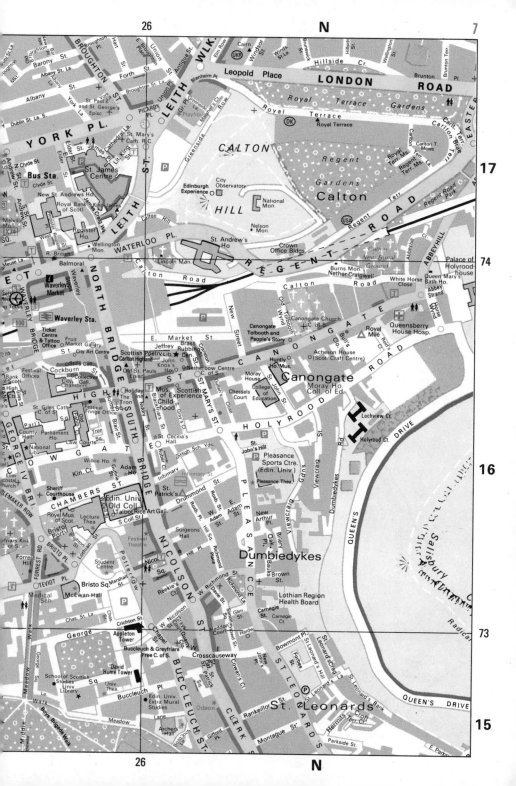

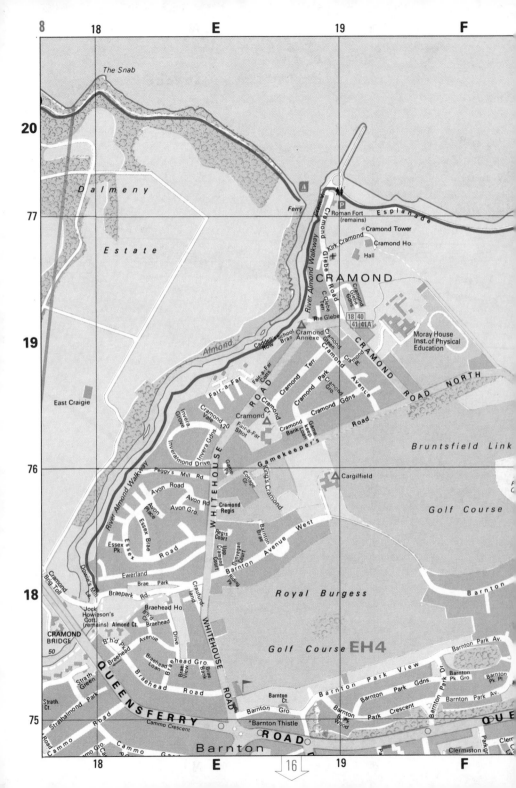

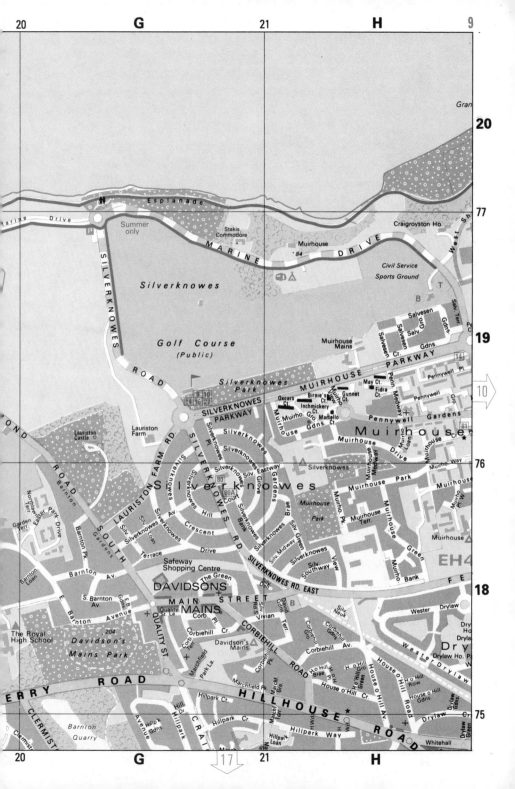

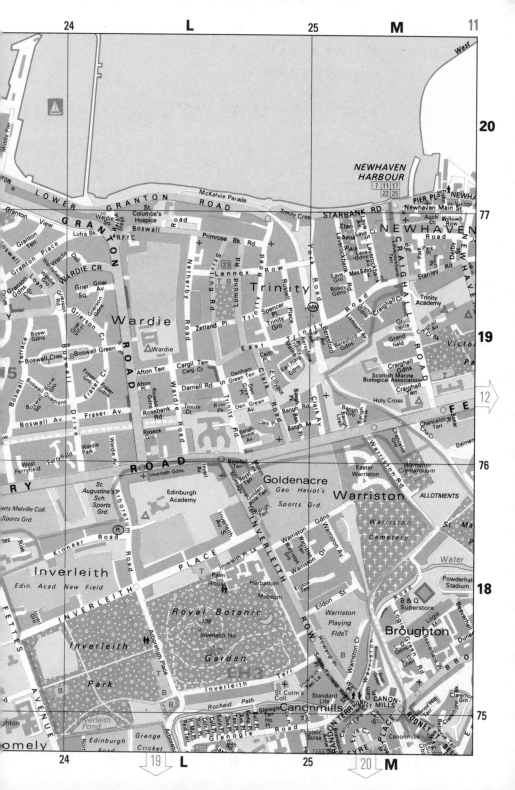

20

West

NEWHAVEN
HARBOUR

7 | 11 | 17
22 | 25

Middle Pier

LOWER   GRANTON   ROAD

McKelvie Parade

Trinity Cres

STARBANK RD.

PIER PL

Newhaven Main St

NEWHA

Victoria

77

Granton View

Granton Terr.

Granton Place

Wardie Dell

GRANTON

St. Columba's Hospice

Boswall

Lufra Bk.

R.F.Y.C.

Primrose Bk. Rd.

NEWHAVEN

Auch

Willowby Row

Road

Star

Lavebank

Laverockbank

Lave Cr.

Laverockbank Park

Laverockbank Terr.

Lave. Gdns Cr.

Bk. Pk.

Park Pl

South Pl

Stanley

CRAIGHALL

Trinity Academy

RD

Granton Loan

Granton Gdns

Grierson Gdns

Grier. Av.

Grier. Sq.

Grierson Villas

Grierson Cr.

WARDIE CR.

Wardie Sq.

Netherby Road

23

Lennox

Lomond Rd

Russell

Trinity

Row

TB

Spencer Pl

Trinity Gro.

Lave. Rd

May.Gdns

Rosev Gdns

Road

Grand field

Craighall Cr.

Gr. ville

Craighall Cr. Bk.

Victor

Pa

19

Boswall Terrace

Bosw. Gdns

Boswall Cres.

Boswall Green

Fraser Gro

Fraser Gdns

Fraser Ct.

Wardie

Wardie

WARDIE

Zetland Pl

East

Trinity Grove

Russell Place

Caith. Pl.

E. Clifton

Earl Haig Gdns

Beresford

Beresford Gdns

Craighall Gdns

Scottish Marine Biological Association

Craighall Terr.

Holy Cross

FE

Boswall Quadrant

Boswall Bosw Gro

Afton Terr.

Carg. Ct.

Cargil Terr.

Denham Green Terr.

Den.Green Av.

Bangh.
Pk.

Bangh. Gro Road

Bangh. Bro'd Loan

Chancelot Terr.

Chu.Ct.

12

Fraser Av.

Boswall Av.

Afton Pl.

Afton Terr.

Rosebk. Gdns

Darnell Rd.

Rosebank Rd.

Trinity Ct.

Den. Green Pk.

Trinity Rd.

Clark Road

Bangh. Bk. Rd

Bangh. Terr.

Clark Av.

Chancelot Gro

Dalmen

Wardie Av.

Wardie Park.

Rosebk Gro.

Rosebk Gro.

Bangh. Bowal Rd.

Clark Pl.

Bangh. Av.

WARRISTON RD.

West Ferryfield

Ferryfield

ROAD

Bowhill Terr.

Inverl. Gdns.

Inverl. Row

Royst Terr.

Montrou

Easter Warriston

Warriston Crematorium

76

Inverleith Gdns.

St. Augustine's Sch. Sports Grd.

Edinburgh Academy Sports Grd.

Goldenacre

Geo. Heriot's

Sports Grd.

Golden acre Terr.

Bangh. Terr.

WARRISTON

ALLOTMENTS

arts Melville Coll.

Sports Grd.

Arboretum

Kinnear Road

PL

Inverleith Av.

Inverleith Av. S

INVERLEITH

PLACE

ROW

Warriston Gdns

Warriston Gr.

Warriston Terr

Warriston Av.

Warriston

Cemetery

St. Ma

P

Water

18

Inverleith

Edin. Acad. New Field

INVERLEITH

Inverleith Pl La

Palm House

Herbarium

Museum

Warriston Dr.

Eildon Terr.

Eildon St.

Warriston Playing Flds T

Powderhall Stadium

B & Q Superstore

Logie

Mill

Broughton

Beaverhall

FETTES

Inverleith

Park

Arboretum Place

Royal Botanic

108

Inverleith Ho.

Garden

St Colm's Coll

Inverleith Terr.

Howard Pl

Warriston Cr.

Warriston

Road

B

Logie Green Rd.

Logie Green Loan

Dune

BRO

AVENUE

Inverleith Pond

Rocheid Path

Glenogle

Glenogle

Inverleith Terr.

Canonmills

Standard Life

CANON
MILLS

CANON MILLS

RODNEY ST

Heriot Hill

Claremon Gro.

Belleview Terr.

75

omely

ghton

Edinburgh Acad

Grange Cricket

Glenogle Road

Philatelic Bureau

EYRE

EYRE

PLACE

Canonmills

Conb

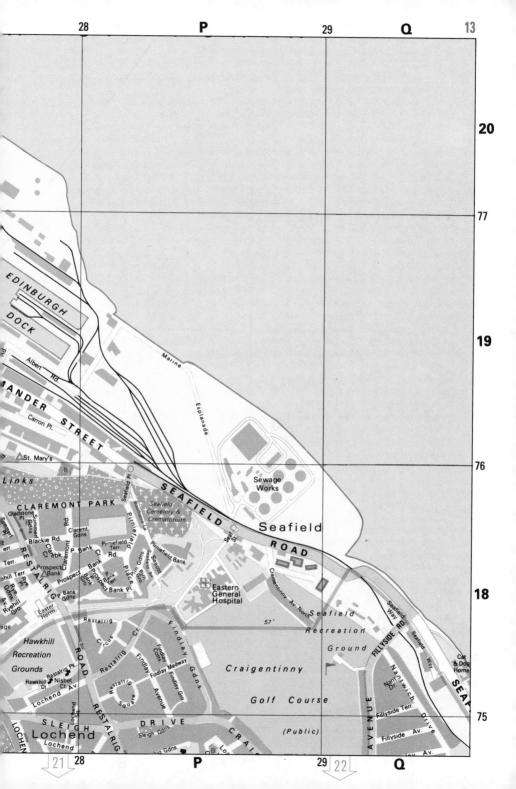

20

77

EDINBURGH

DOCK

Albert Rd

Marine

Esplanade

MANDER STREET

Carron Pl.

St. Mary's

19

Links

B

76

Seafield Cemetery & Crematorium

Sewage Works

Seafield

CLAREMONT PARK

Gladstone Pl

Summer Gdns

Claremt. Gdns

Blackie Rd.

Claremt.

P. Bank Ct

Pirniefield Terr.

Rd.

Claremont

Pirniefield Bank

Pirniefield Place

Pirniefield Gdns

Pirniefield Gro

Sleaford Av.

Prospect Bank

SEAFIELD

Sea St.

ROAD

Terr.

RESTALRIG

P. Bank

P Bank Gro.

P Bank Terr

Prospect

Prospect

Bank Pl.

Bank Gdns.

Rye...

Ryehill Terr.

Ryehill

Gdns.

Ryehill

Gro.

age

Easter

Term.

Craigentinny Av. North

Eastern General Hospital

Seafield

57

Recreation

Seafield Way

FILLSIDE RD

18

Hawkhill

Recreation

Grounds

RESTALRIG

ROAD

Restalrig

Circus

Ct.

Restalrig

Restalrig

Square

Findlay

Gdns.

Findlay

Cotts.

Findlay Medway

Findlay Gro

Findlay Gdns.

Findlay Avenue

Ground

Craigentinny

Golf Course

Nantwich Dr.

Nantwich Drive

Seafield Way

Cat & Dog Home

SEA

Hawkhill Ct.

Nisbet Ct. Av.

Lochend

Lochend

SLEIGH DRIVE

Lochend

Sleigh Gdns

RESTALRIG

CRAIG

Restalrig Gdns

Lochend

75

(Public)

AVENUE

Fillside Terr.

Fillyside Av.

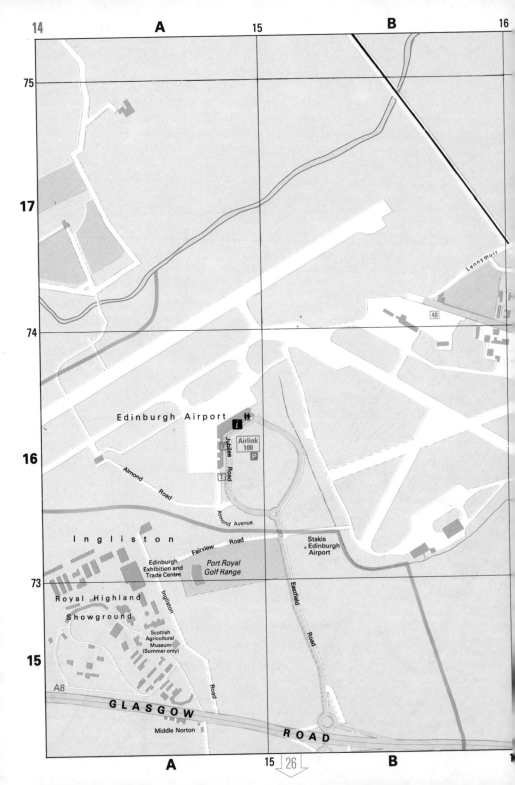

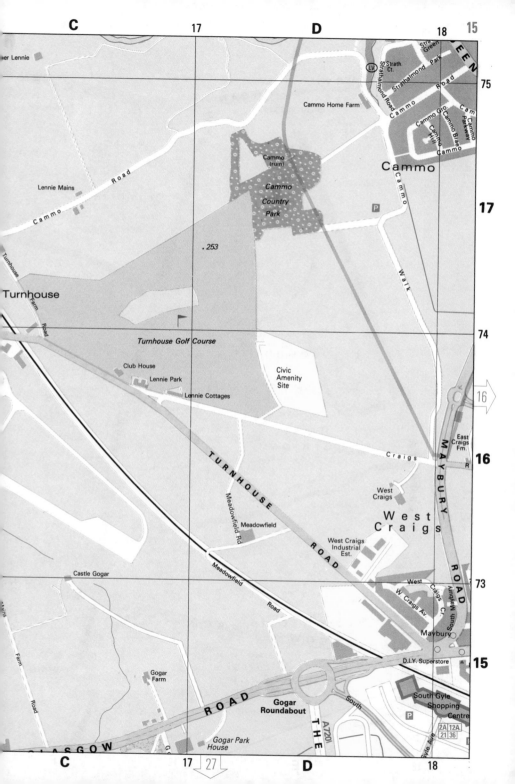

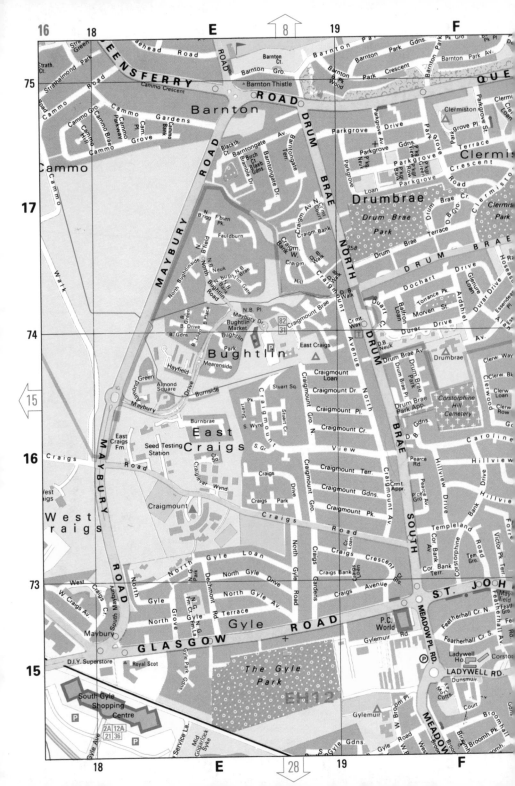

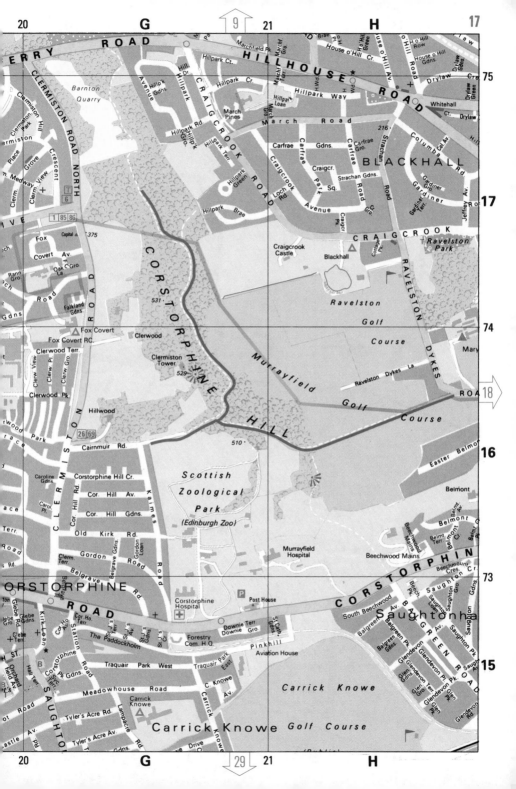

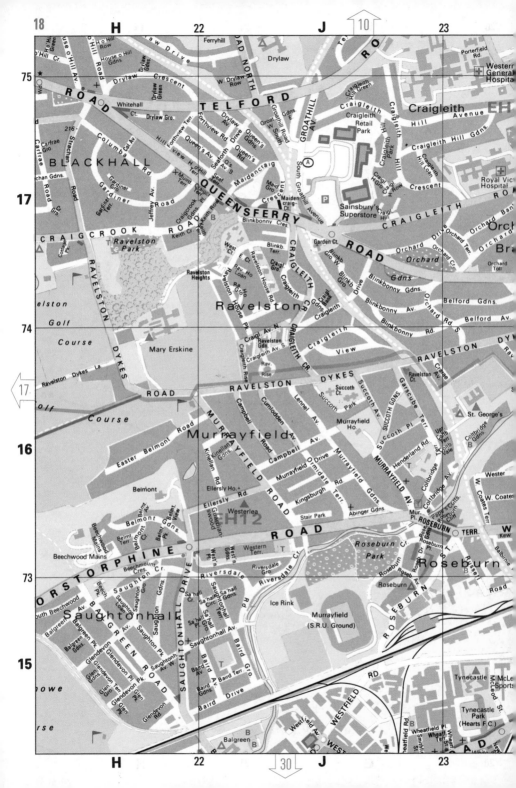

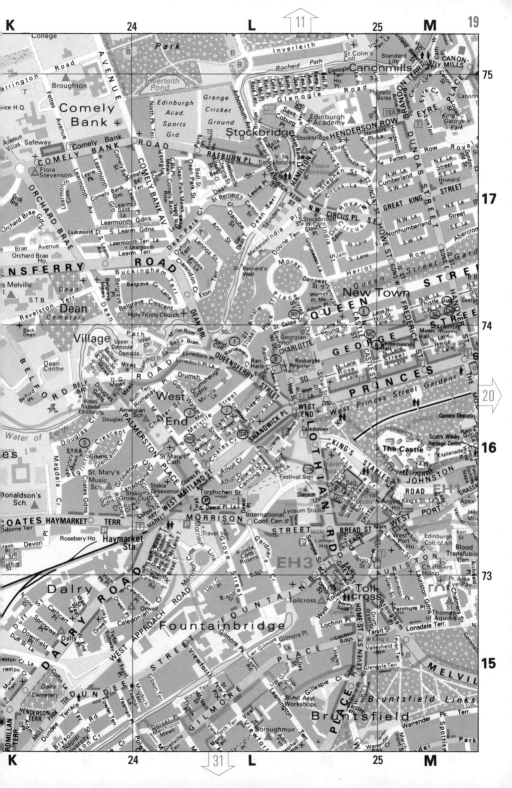

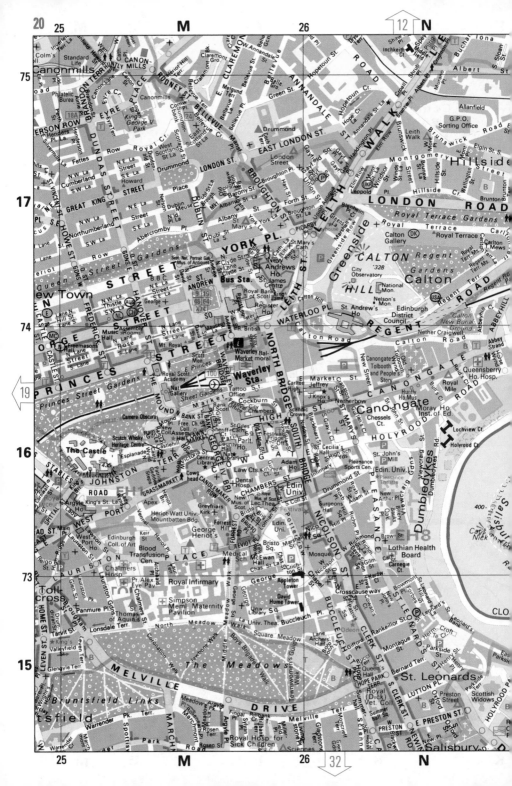

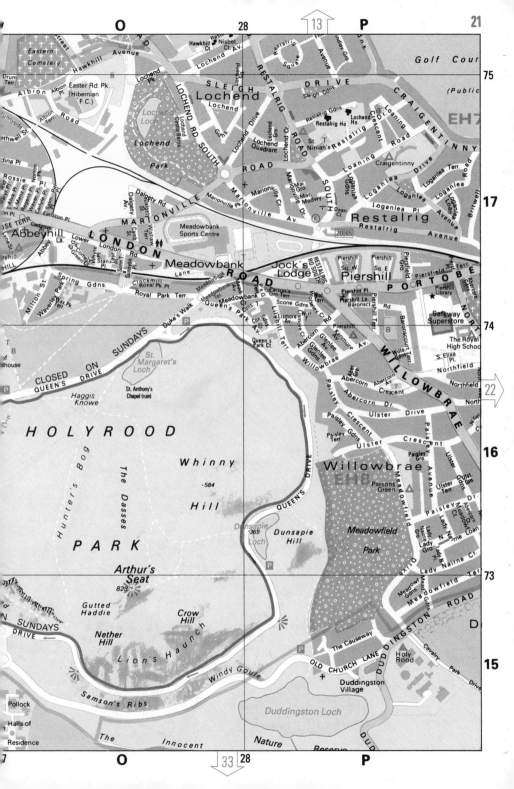

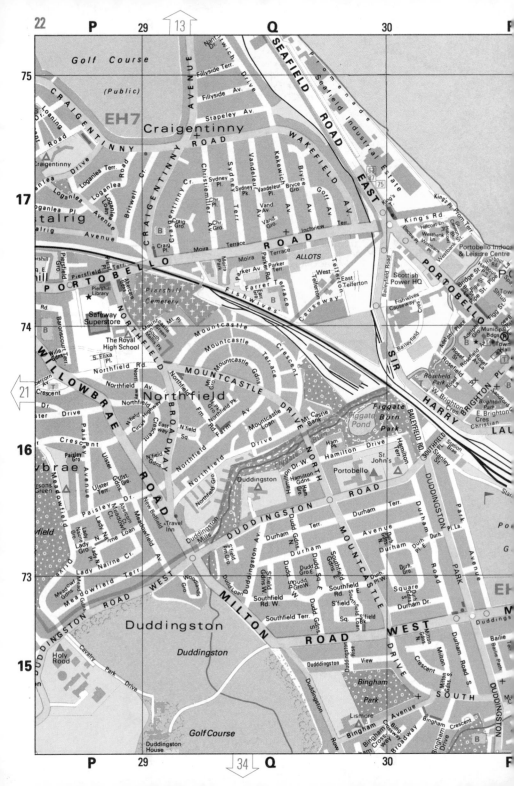

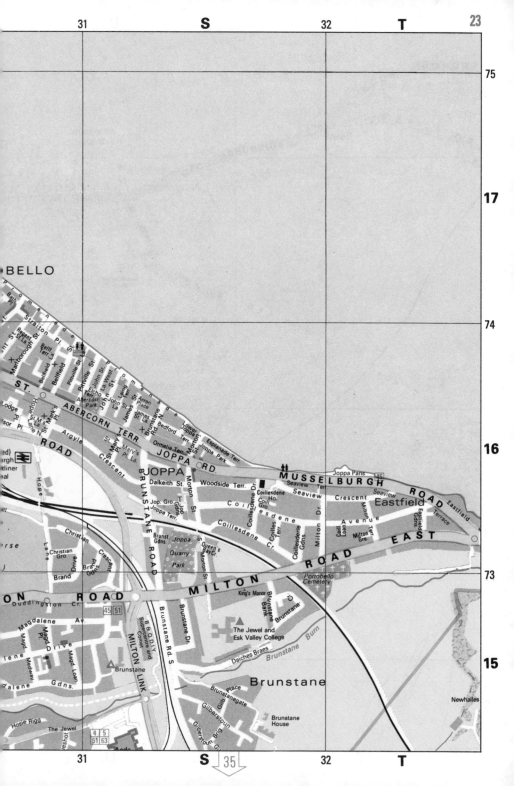

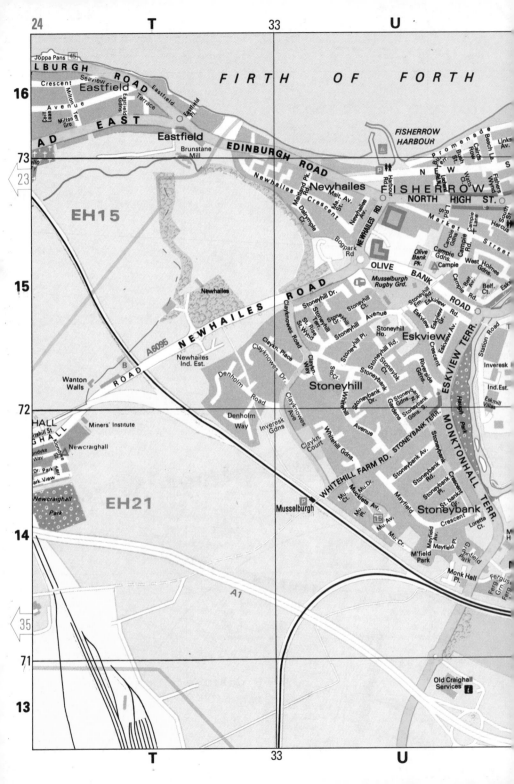

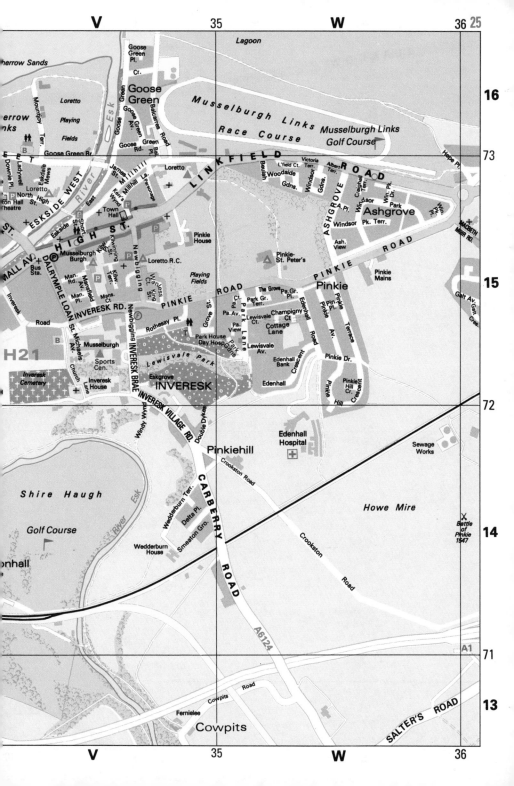

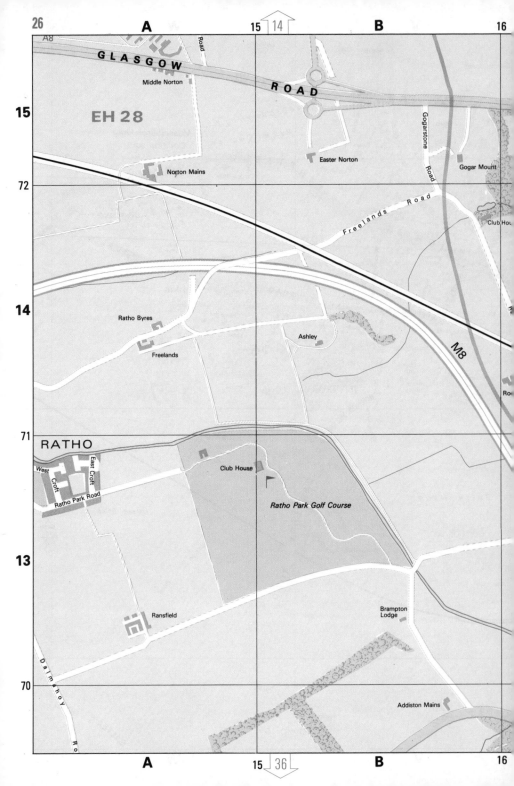

GLASGOW   ROAD

Gogar
Roundabout

Gogar Park
House

Gogar Park
Curling Club

Gogarburn
Hospital

Gogarburn Hospital

THE CITY OF EDINBURGH BYPASS

A720

South

Gyle Ave

Lochside

Lochside

Edin.

Gyle

Gyle Ave

Park

Lochside

South Gyle
Shopping
Centre

P

2A 12A
21 36

Scottish
Equitable

Cres.

E d i n b u r g

P a r k

I n d u s t

E s t

15

72

14

28

71

13

70

rn Golf Course

Gogar

Station   Road

Millburn Tower

Kellerstane

Gogarburn
Farm

Gogarbank

Over Gogar

Trefoil School

Hermiston House Road

Union Canal

West
Hermiston

Wester Row

Hermiston
House

Mid Hermiston

Long
Hermiston

RICCARTON

CALDER   ROAD

Heriot Watt
Research
Park

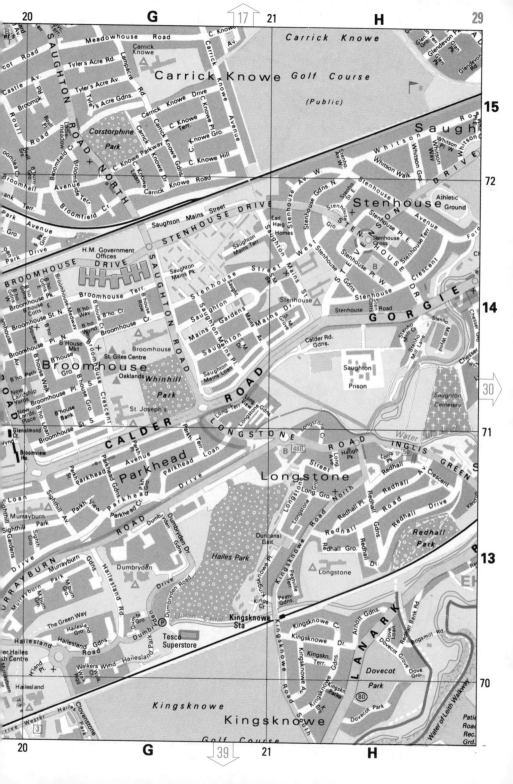

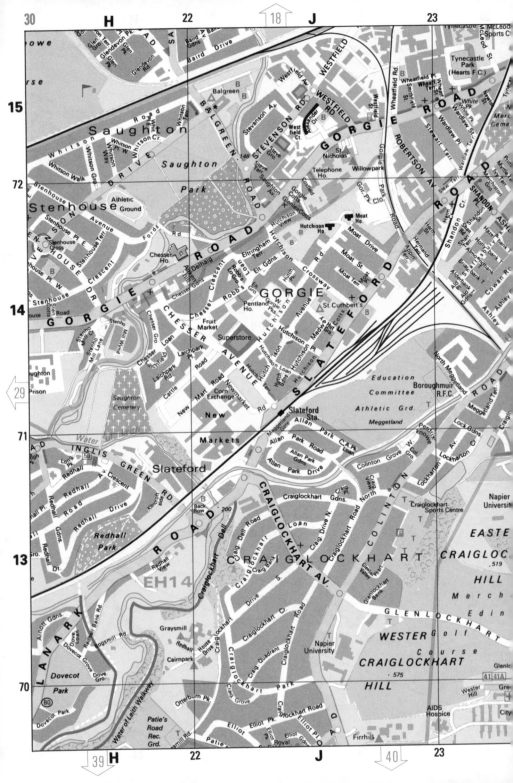

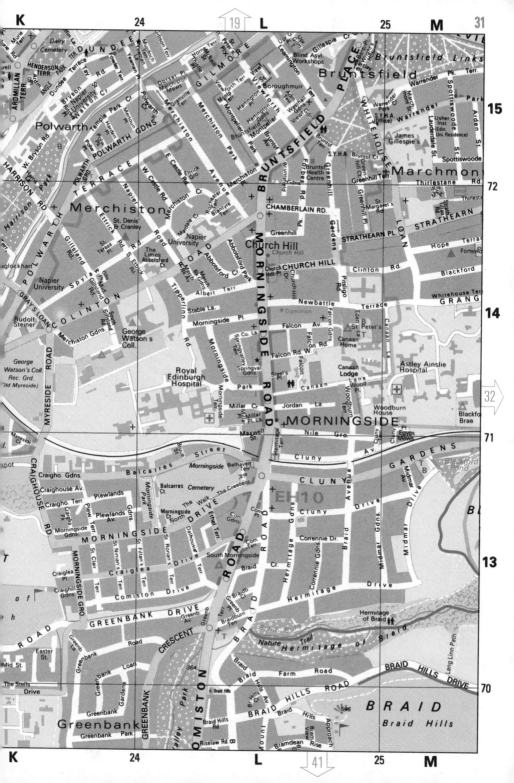

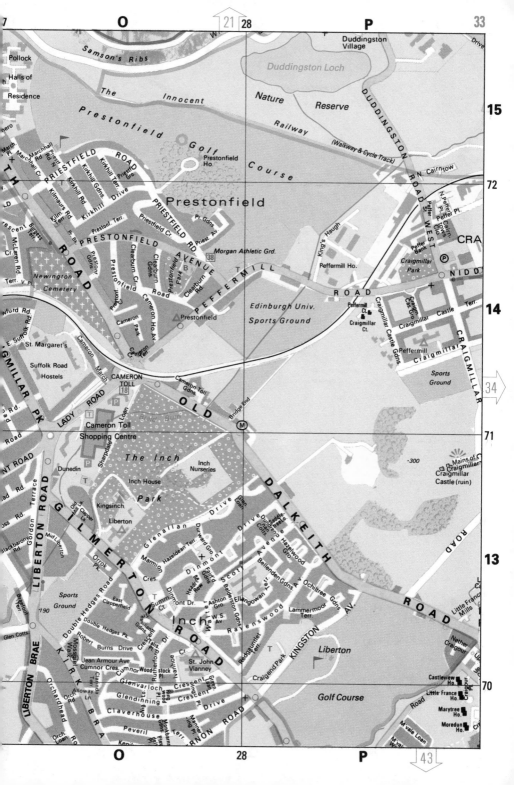

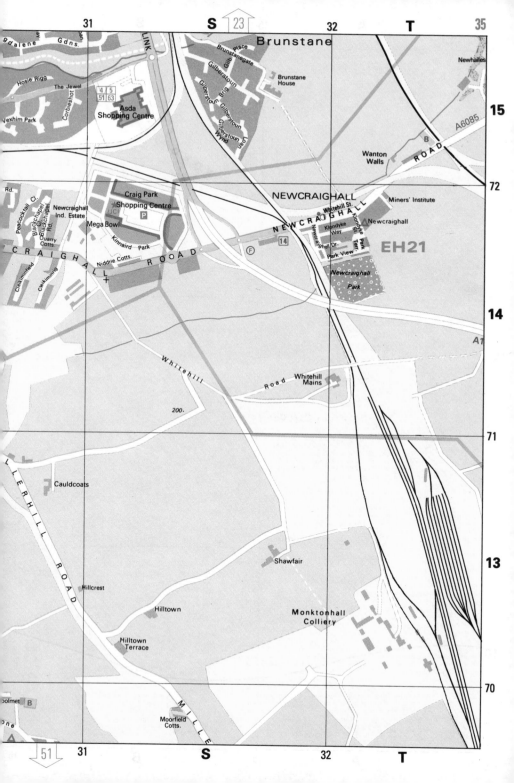

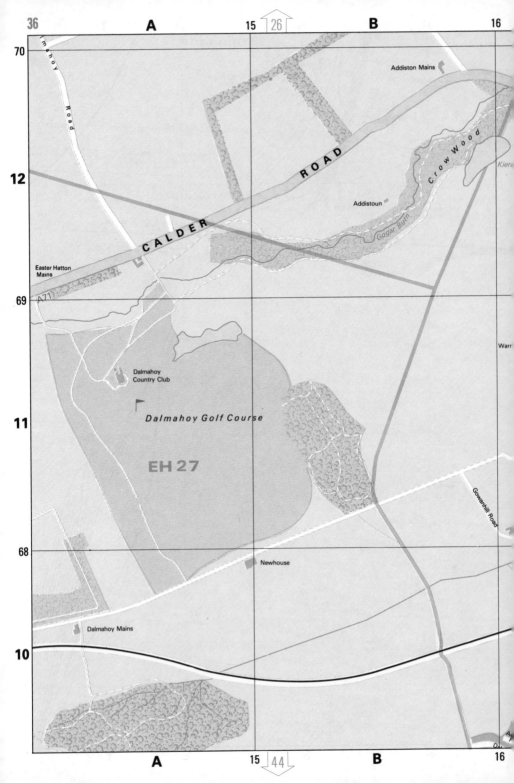

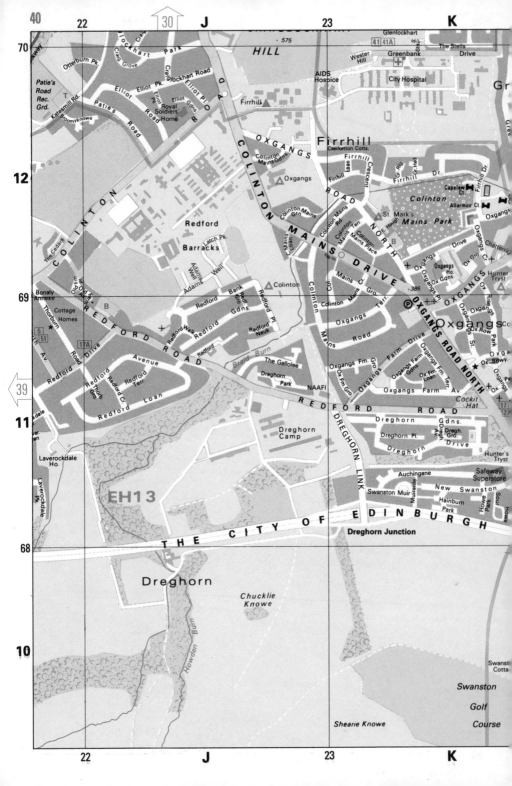

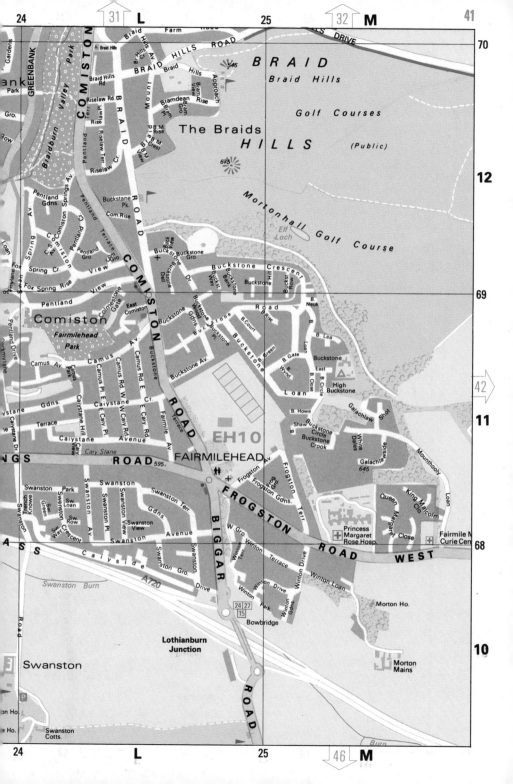

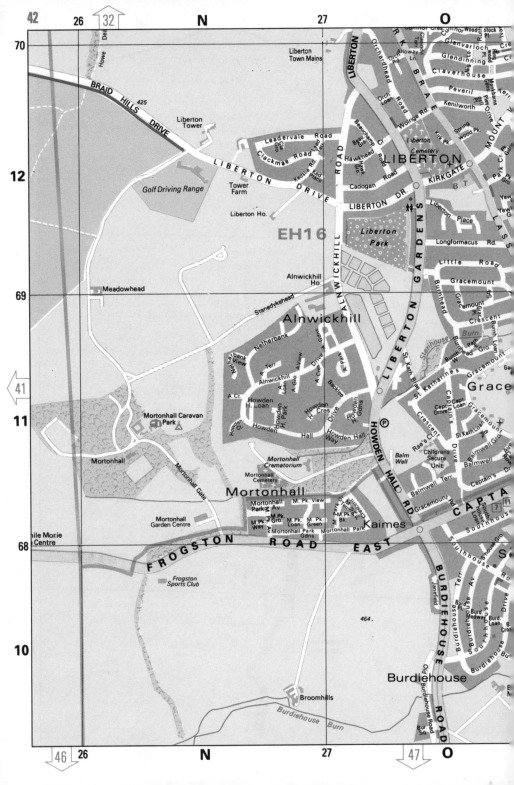

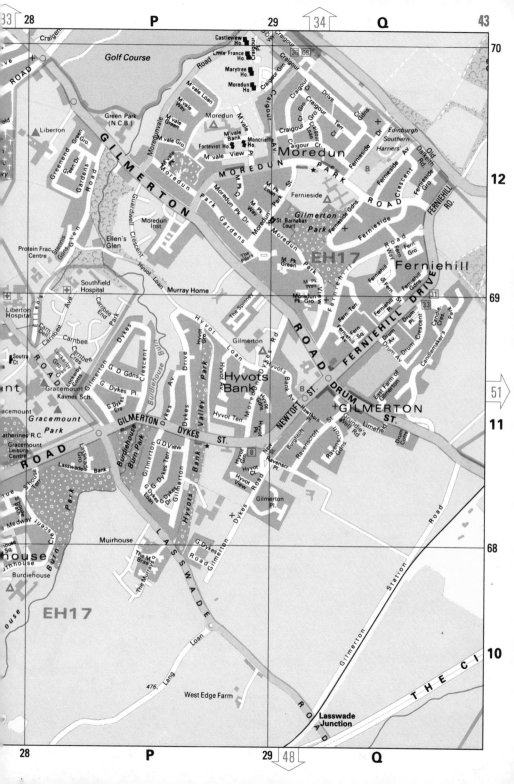

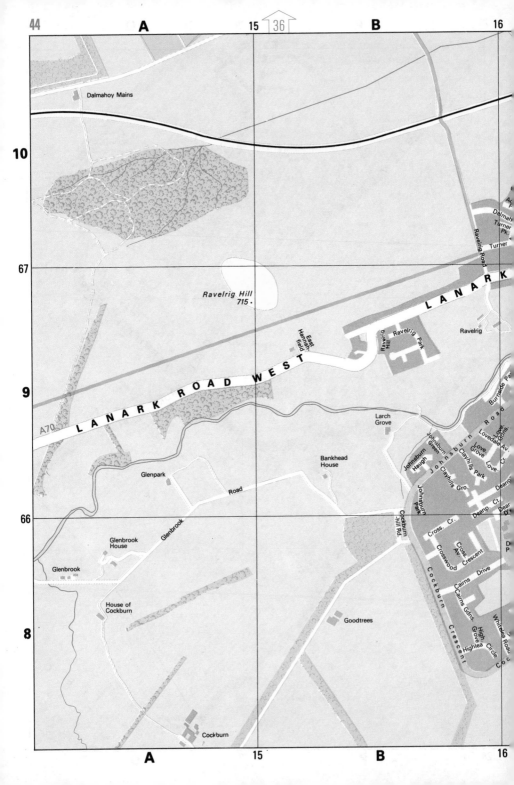

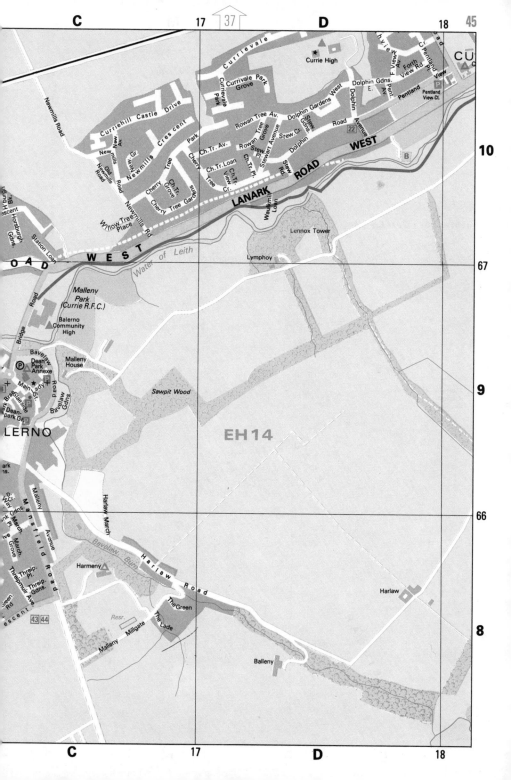

Currievale

Currievale Park Grove

Currievale Park

Curriehill Castle Drive

Crescent

Cherry Tree Park

New Av.
New Gr.
Newmills
Old Newmills Road

Newmills Road

Newmills Road

New Newmills Road

Cherry Tree Grove

Cherry Tree Gdns.

Cherry Tree Garden

Willow Tree Place

Newmills Rd.

Station Loan

Bridge Road

Ch.Tr.
Loan

Ch.Tr. Av.

Rowan Tree Av.

Rowan Tree

Rowan Tree Grove

Ch.Tr. Av.
Ch.Tr. Loan
Ch.Tr. Tree
Ch.Tr.
Cr.

Ch.Tr. Pl.
Ch.Tr. View

Stew Ct.

Stewart Avenue

Stewart Avenue

Waukmill Loan

Dolphin Gardens West

Dolphin Gardens E.

Stew.
Gdns.

Dolphin

Road

Avenue

Dolphin

Stew
Rd.

22

★ Currie High

Currie High

F. View Av.

Forth View Rd.

Pentl. Av.

Pentland

Ci. Pentland View

Pentland View Ct.

P

B

CU

★ Lennox Tower

LANARK   ROAD   WEST

WEST   ROAD

Water of Leith

Lymphoy

Malleny Park
(Currie R.F.C.)

Balerno Community High

Bavelaw
Dean Park Annexe

Malleny House

Main St.

Bavelaw Gdns.

Sawpit Wood

EH 14

Braeside
Dean Park Gr.

LERNO

ark
ns.

Malleny Way

Mansfield Road

Bank Gdns. March
Threipmuir Grove

Threip. Pl.
Threip. Gdns.
Threipmuir Ave.

escent Rd

43 44

Avenue

Harlaw March

Bavelaw Burn

Harlaw   Road

Harmeny ▲

The Green

Resr.

Malleny

Millgate

The Lade

The Green

Harlaw

Balleny

Horsburgh Bk.
Horsburgh Gdns.

O A D

10

67

9

66

8

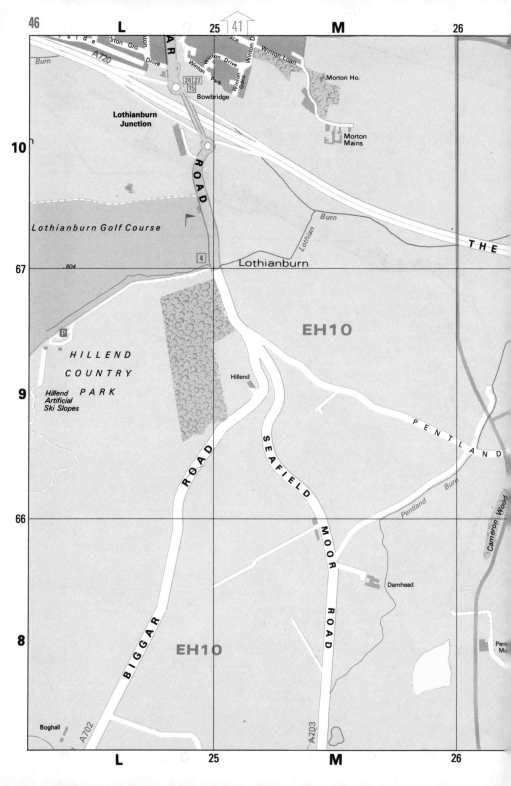

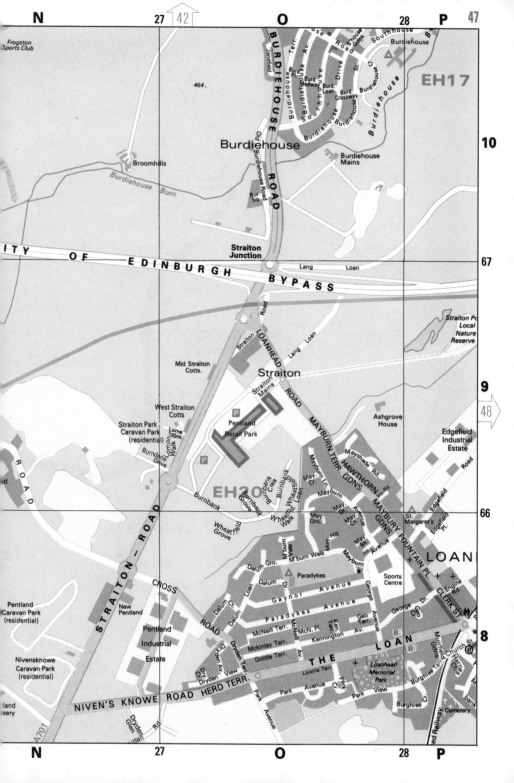

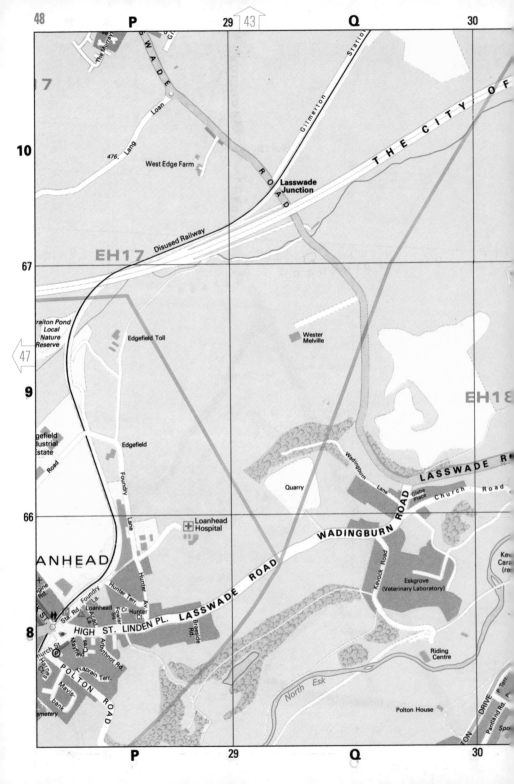

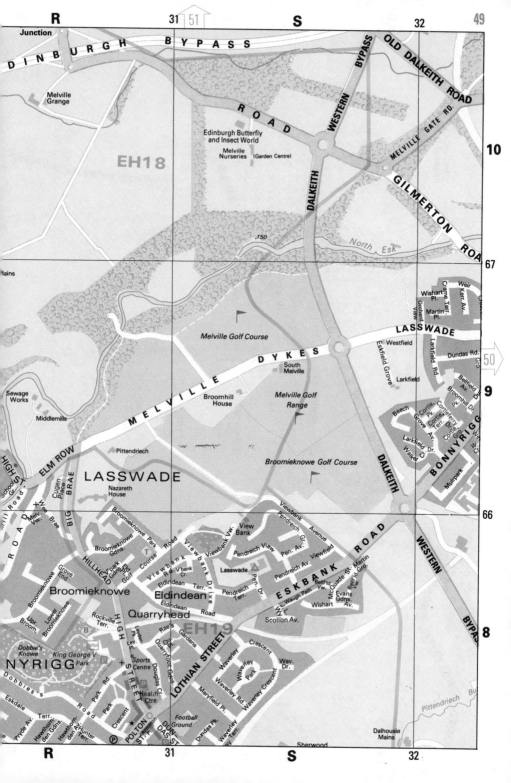

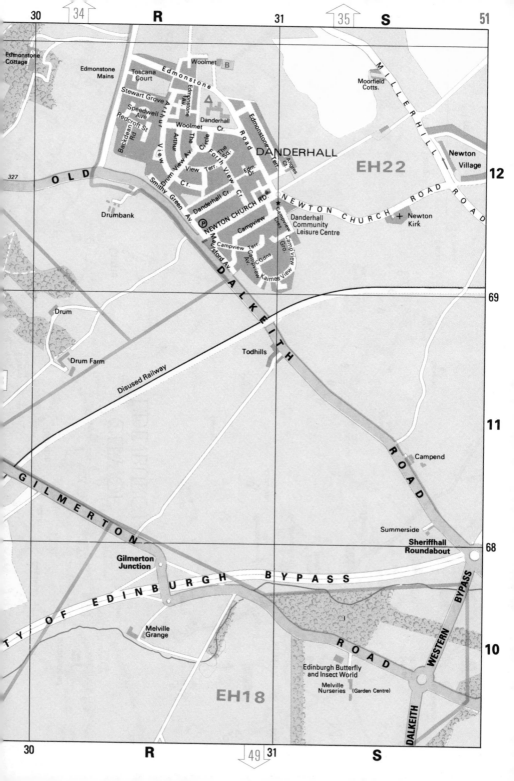

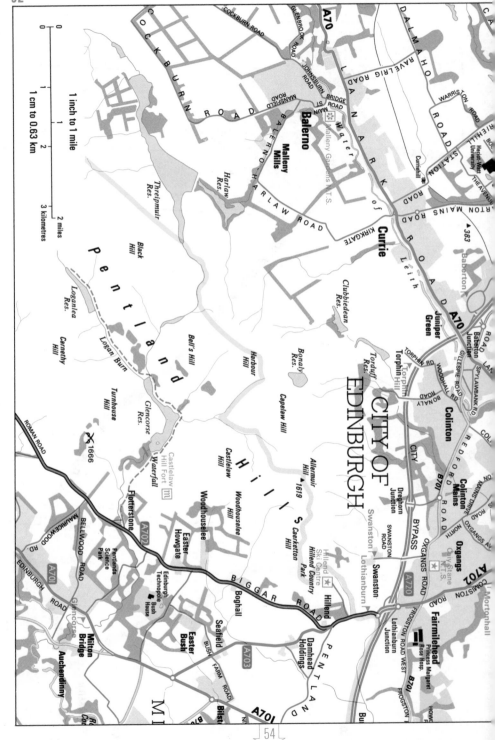

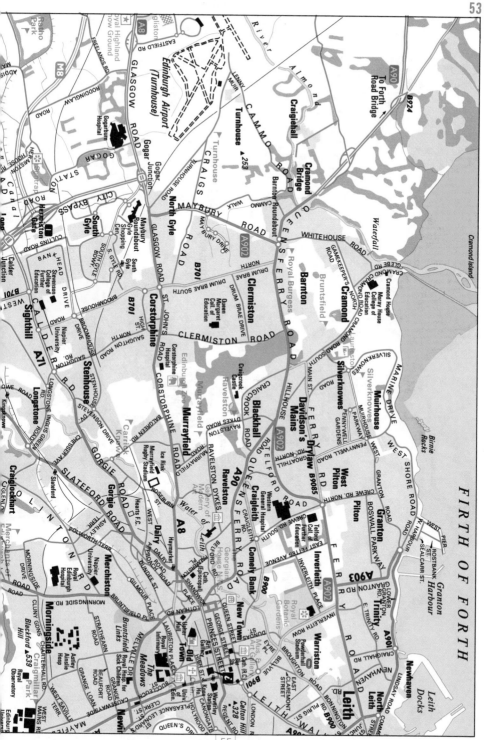

MIDLOTHIAN

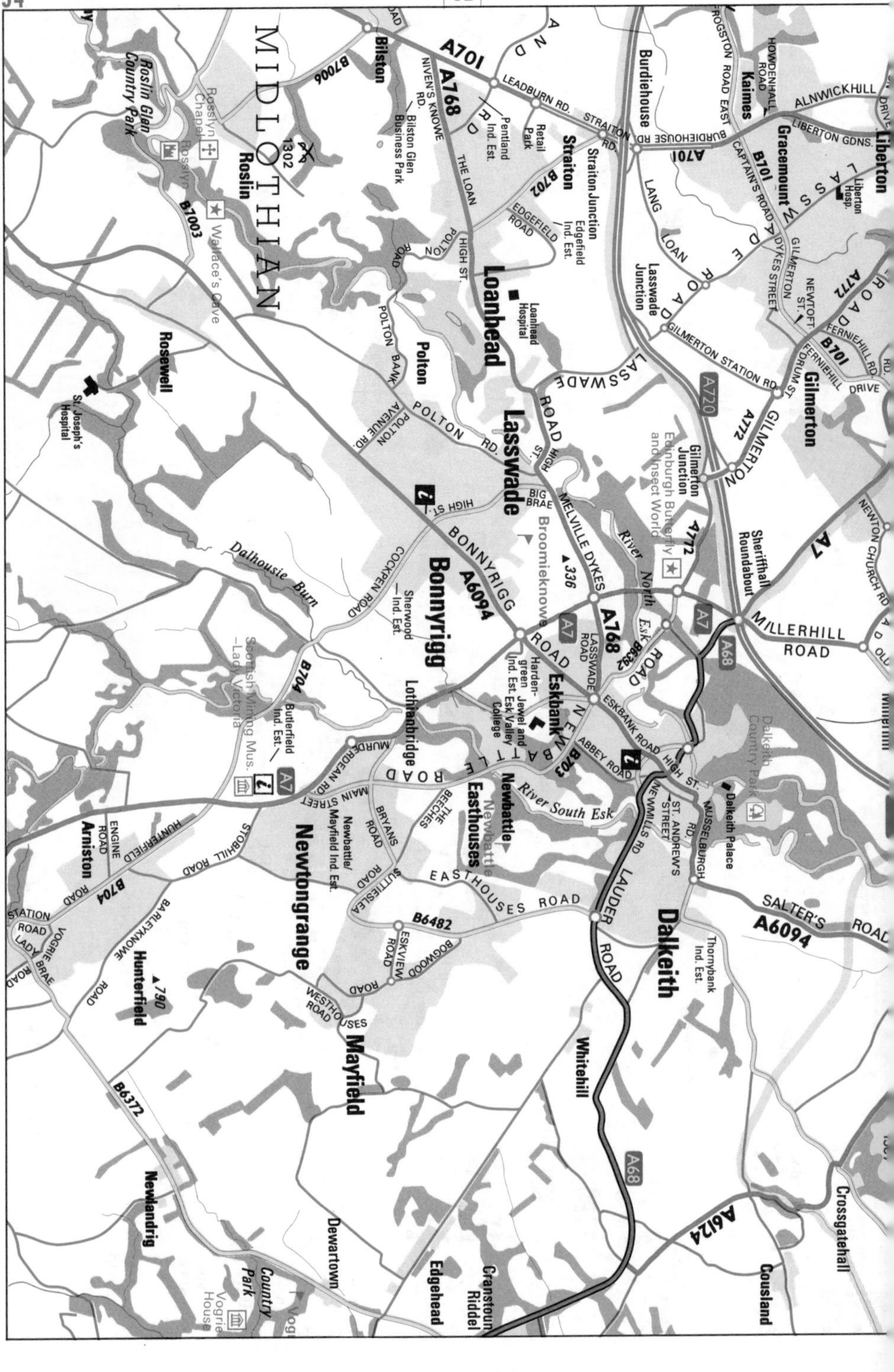

Roslin Glen Country Park

Rosslyn Chapel

B7006

Bilston

A701

A768

A701

LEADBURN RD

STRAITON RD

NIVEN'S KNOWE RD.

Pentland Ind. Est.

Retail Park

Straiton

B7003

THE LOAN

HIGH ST.

EDGEFIELD ROAD

Straiton Junction

Edgefield Ind. Est.

Burdiehouse

BURDIEHOUSE RD.

LANG

LOAN

A701

FROGSTON ROAD EAST

HOWDENHALL ROAD

ALNWICKHILL

Kaimes

LIBERTON GDNS

Gracemount

CAPTAIN'S ROAD

B701

NEWTOFT ST.

GILMERTON

DYKES STREET

Liberton

Liberton Hosp.

A772

FERNIEHILL RD

FERNIEHILL DRIVE

Roslin

1302

Bilston Glen Business Park

Rosewell

St Joseph's Hospital

B1003

Wallace's Cave

POLTON ROAD

POLTON BANK

POLTON AVENUE RD.

Polton

Loanhead Hospital

Loanhead

Lasswade

HIGH ST.

BIG BRAE

Lasswade Junction

GILMERTON STATION RD.

Gilmerton Junction

Gilmerton

A772

A720

A772

GILMERTON

NEWTON CHURCH RD.

Dalhousie Burn

COCKPEN ROAD

Bonnyrigg

A6094

BONNYRIGG ROAD

Sherwood Ind. Est.

Broomieknowe

MELVILLE DYKES

▲336

River North Esk

Edinburgh Butterfly and Insect World

Sheriffhall Roundabout

A7

MILLERHILL ROAD

NEWTON

B704

Butterfield Ind. Est.

Scottish Mining Mus — Lady Victoria

B704

Lothianbridge

MURDERDEAN RD.

MAIN STREET

Harden-green Ind. Est. Esk Valley College

Jewel and Esk Valley College

NEWBATTLE

LASSWADE ROAD

Eskbank

B6392

A768

A7

ESKBANK ROAD

HIGH ST.

Dalkeith Palace

Dalkeith Country Park

ST. ANDREW'S STREET

MUSSELBURGH

A68

Arniston

ENGINE ROAD

HUNTERFIELD ROAD

STOBHILL ROAD

STATION ROAD

LADY BRAE

VOGRIE ROAD

BALLEYKNOWE

B704

Newtongrange

Newbattle/Mayfield Ind. Est.

BRYANS ROAD

RUTHERSIDE

SUTTIESLEA

THE BEECHES

Newbattle

River South Esk

ST. ANDREW'S

ABBEY ROAD

B703

NE WILLS RD

LAUDER ROAD

Dalkeith

SALTER'S ROAD

A6094

Thornybank Ind. Est.

Hunterfield

▲790

ESKVIEW ROAD

BOGWOOD ROAD

WESTHOUSES ROAD

B6482

EASTHOUSES ROAD

Easthouses

Mayfield

Whitehill

A68

B6372

Newlandrig

Dewartown

Edgehead

Cranston Riddel

Cousland

Crossgatehall

Country Park

Vogrie House

INDEX TO STREETS

General Abbreviations

Acad.	Academy	Ct.	Court	Ho.	House	R.F.C.	Rugby Football Club
All.	Alley	Cts.	Courts	Hos.	Houses	Rd.	Road
App.	Approach	Dr.	Drive	Hosp.	Hospital	Ri.	Rise
Arc.	Arcade	E.	East	Ind.	Industrial	S.	South
Av.	Avenue	Esp.	Esplanade	Junct.	Junction	Sch.	School
Bdy.	Broadway	Est.	Estate	La.	Lane	Sq.	Square
Bk.	Bank	Ex.	Exchange	Ln.	Loan	St.	Street, Saint
Bldgs.	Buildings	Fld.	Field	Lo.	Lodge	Sta.	Station
Bri.	Bridge	Flds.	Fields	Lwr.	Lower	Ter.	Terrace
Cem.	Cemetery	Fm.	Farm	Mem.	Memorial	Twr.	Tower
Cen.	Centre	G.P.O.	General Post Office	Mkt.	Market	Vills.	Villas
Cft.	Croft	Gall.	Gallery	Ms.	Mews	Vw.	View
Ch.	Church	Gdn.	Garden	Mt.	Mount	W.	West
Circ.	Circle	Gdns.	Gardens	N.	North	Wd.	Wood
Clo.	Close	Gra.	Grange	Par.	Parade	Wds.	Woods
Coll.	College	Grd.	Ground	Pk.	Park	Wf.	Wharf
Cor.	Corner	Grn.	Green	Pl.	Place	Wr.	Wester
Cotts.	Cottages	Grns.	Greens	Pt.	Port	Yd.	Yard
Crem.	Crematorium	Gro.	Grove	Quad.	Quadrant		
Cres.	Crescent	H.Q.	Head Quarters	R.C.	Roman Catholic		

Post Town Abbreviations

NB. All entries are for Edinburgh Post Town unless otherwise stated.

Bal.	Balerno	Jun.Grn.	Juniper Green	Muss.	Musselburgh
Bonny.	Bonnyrigg	Lass.	Lasswade	Newbr.	Newbridge
Dalk.	Dalkeith	Loanh.	Loanhead		

District Abbreviations

				Ricc.	Riccarton
Cram.	Cramond	Inglis.	Ingliston	Strai.	Straiton
Dand.	Danderhall	Inver.	Inveresk	White.	Whitecraig
David.	Davidsons Mains	Monk.	Monktonhall	Wool.	Woolmet
Easth.	Easthouses	Newcr.	Newcraighall		

Abbey La. EH8	21	O17	Aitkenhill EH11	30	H14	Alnwickhill Gro. EH16	42	N11
Abbey Rd., Dalk. EH22	50	T9	Alan Breck Gdns. EH4	16	F17	Alnwickhill Ln. EH16	42	N11
Abbey Strand EH8	7	N16	Albany La. EH1	7	M17	Alnwickhill Pk. EH16	42	O11
Abbey St. EH7	21	O17	Albany St. EH1	7	M17	Alnwickhill Rd. EH16	42	O11
Montrose Ter.			Albany St. La. EH1	7	M17	Alnwickhill Ter. EH16	42	N11
Abbeyhill EH8	7	N16	Albert Pl. EH7	20	N17	Alnwickhill Vw. EH16	42	N11
Abbeyhill Cres. EH8	7	N17	Albert Rd. EH6	13	O19	Alva Pl. EH7	21	O17
Abbeymount EH8	20	N17	Albert St. EH7	12	N18	Alva St. EH2	6	L16
Abbotsford Ct. EH10	31	L14	Albert Ter. EH10	31	L14	Alvanley Ter. EH9	31	L15
Abbotsford Cres. EH10	31	L14	Albert Ter., Muss. EH21	25	W15	*Whitehouse Ln.*		
Abbotsford Pk. EH10	31	L14	Albion Pl. EH7	21	O17	Anchorfield EH6	12	N19
Abercorn Av. EH8	21	P16	Albion Rd. EH7	21	O17	*Lindsay Rd.*		
Abercorn Cotts. EH15	21	P15	Albion Ter. EH7	21	O17	Ancrum Bk., Dalk. EH22	50	T9
The Causeway			Albyn Pl. EH2	6	L17	Ancrum Rd., Dalk. EH22	50	T9
Abercorn Ct. EH8	21	P16	Alcorn Rigg EH14	39	G12	Anderson Pl. EH6	12	N19
Abercorn Cres. EH8	21	P16	Alderbank Gdns. EH11	30	K14	Andrew Wd. Ct. EH6	11	M19
Abercorn Dr. EH8	21	P16	Alderbank Pl. EH11	30	K14	*Newhaven Main St.*		
Abercorn Gdns. EH8	22	P17	Alderbank Ter. EH11	30	K14	Angle Pk. Ter. EH11	19	K15
Abercorn Gro. EH8	21	P16	Alexander Dr. EH11	30	J15	Angres Ct. (Dand.), Dalk. EH22	51	S12
Abercorn Rd. EH8	21	P16	Alfred Pl. EH9	32	N14	Ann St. EH4	6	L17
Abercorn Ter. EH15	23	R16	Allan Pk. Cres. EH14	30	J14	Annandale St. EH7	20	M17
Abercromby Pl. EH3	6	M17	Allan Pk. Dr. EH14	30	J13	Annandale St. La. EH7	20	N17
Abinger Gdns. EH12	18	J16	Allan Pk. Gdns. EH14	30	J13	Annfield EH6	12	M19
Academy La., Loanh. EH20	48	P8	Allan Pk. Ln. EH14	30	J13	Annfield St. EH6	12	M19
Academy Pk. EH6	12	O18	Allan Pk. Rd. EH14	30	J13	Antigua St. EH1	7	N17
Academy St. EH6	12	O18	Allan St. EH4	19	L17	Anworth Vills. EH12	29	G15
Adams Well EH13	40	J12	Allan Ter., Dalk. EH22	50	U10	*Saughton Rd. N.*		
Addiston Cres., Bal. EH14	44	C10	Allandale EH11	39	H11	Appin Ter. EH14	30	J14
Addiston Gro., Bal. EH14	44	C10	*Spylaw St.*			Arboretum Av. EH4	19	L17
Addiston Pk., Bal. EH14	44	C10	Allanfield EH7	20	N17	Arboretum Pl. EH3	11	L18
Adelphi Gro. EH15	22	R16	Allermuir Ct. EH13	40	K12	Arboretum Rd. EH3	11	L18
Adelphi Pl. EH15	22	R16	Allermuir Rd. EH13	39	H11	Arbuthnot Rd., Loanh. EH20	48	P8
Admiral Ter. EH10	31	L15	Alloway Ln. EH16	42	O12	Archibald Pl. EH3	6	M16
Admiralty St. EH6	12	N19	Almond Av. EH12	14	A16	Arden St. EH9	32	M15
Advocates Clo. EH1	7	M16	Almond Bk. Cotts. EH4	8	E18	Ardmillan Pl. EH11	31	K15
High St.			*Whitehouse Rd.*			Ardmillan Ter. EH11	31	K15
Affleck Ct. EH12	16	E16	Almond Ct. EH4	8	E18	Ardmillan Ter. La. EH11	31	K15
Craigievar Wynd			Almond Ct. EH16	34	Q14	*Ardmillan Ter.*		
Afton Pl. EH5	11	L19	Almond Grn. EH12	16	E16	Ardshiel Av. EH4	16	F17
Afton Ter. EH5	11	L19	Almond Rd. EH12	14	A16	Argyle Cres. EH15	23	R16
Agnew Ter. EH6	12	M19	Almond Sq. EH12	16	E16	Argyle Pk. Ter. EH9	20	M15
Connaught Pl.			Almondbank Ter. EH11	30	K14	Argyle Pl. EH9	20	M15
Ainslie Pl. EH3	6	L17	Alnwickhill Ct. EH16	42	N11	Argyle St. EH6	12	N19
Airlie Pl. EH3	20	M17	Alnwickhill Cres. EH16	42	N11	Argyll Ter. EH11	19	L16
Aitchison's Pl. EH15	22	R17	Alnwickhill Dr. EH16	42	N11	Arniston Pl., Bonny. EH19	49	R8
Figgate St.			Alnwickhill Gdns. EH16	42	N11	Arnott Gdns. EH14	29	H13

Name	Page	Grid
Blacket Pl. EH9	32	N15
Blackford Av. EH9	32	M14
Blackford Bk. EH9	32	M14
Blackford Glen Rd. EH16	32	N13
Blackford Hill EH9	32	M13
Blackford Hill Gro. EH9	32	M13
Blackford Hill Ri. EH9	32	M13
Blackford Hill Vw. EH9	32	M13
Blackford Rd. EH9	32	M14
Blackfriars St. EH1	7	N16
Blackie Rd. EH6	13	O18
Blackthorn Ct. EH4	16	E17
Blackwood Cres. EH9	32	N15
Blaeberry Gdns. EH4	16	E17
Blair St. EH1	7	M16
Blantyre Ter. EH10	31	L14
Bleachfield EH6	12	M18
Blenheim Pl. EH7	7	N17
Blinkbonny Av. EH4	18	J17
Blinkbonny Cres. EH4	18	J17
Blinkbonny Gdns. EH4	18	J17
Blinkbonny Gro. EH4	18	J17
Blinkbonny Gro. W. EH4	18	J17
Blinkbonny Rd. EH4	18	J17
Blinkbonny Rd., Currie EH14	38	E10
Blinkbonny Ter. EH4	18	J17
Boat Grn. EH3	11	M18
Bogpark Rd., Muss. EH21	24	U15
Bogsmill Rd. EH14	29	H13
Bonaly Av. EH13	39	H11
Bonaly Brae EH13	39	H11
Bonaly Cres. EH13	39	H11
Bonaly Dr. EH13	39	H11
Bonaly Fm. Cotts. EH13	39	H11
Bonaly Gdns. EH13	39	H11
Bonaly Gro. EH13	39	H11
Bonaly Ri. EH13	39	H11
Bonaly Rd. EH13	39	H11
Bonaly Steading EH13	39	H11
Bonaly Ter. EH13	39	H11
Bonaly Wr. EH13	39	H11
Bonar Pl. EH6	11	M19
Bonnington Av. EH6	12	M19
Bonnington Gro. EH6	12	M19
Bonnington Rd. EH6	12	N18
Bonnington Rd. La. EH6	12	N18
Bonnington Ter. EH6	12	M19
Bonnyhaugh EH6	12	M18
Bonnyhaugh La. EH6	12	M18
Bonnyrigg Rd., Dalk. EH22	50	T9
Boothacre Cotts. EH6	13	P18
Seafield Pl.		
Boothacre La. EH6	13	P18
Boroughloch Bldgs. EH8	7	N15
Boroughloch La.		
Boroughloch La. EH8	7	N15
Boroughloch Sq. EH8	7	N15
Boroughloch La.		
Borthwick Pl. EH12	19	K16
Borthwick's Clo. EH1	7	M16
High St.		
Boswall Av. EH5	11	K19
Boswall Cres. EH5	11	K19
Boswall Dr. EH5	11	K19
Boswall Gdns. EH5	11	K19
Boswall Grn. EH5	11	L19
Boswall Gro. EH5	11	K19
Boswall Ln. EH5	11	K19
Boswall Ms. EH5	11	K19
Boswall Ln.		
Boswall Parkway EH5	10	K19
Boswall Pl. EH5	11	K19
Boswall Quad. EH5	11	K19
Boswall Rd. EH5	11	L19
Boswall Sq. EH5	11	K19
Boswall Ter. EH5	11	K19
Bothwell St. EH7	21	N17
Boundary Rd.	37	D12
(Ricc.), Currie EH14		
Bowhill Ter. EH3	11	L18
Bowie's Clo. EH6	12	O19
Bowling Grn., The EH6	12	N19
Bowmont Pl. EH8	7	N15
Boyd's Entry EH1	7	N16
St. Mary's St.		
Boy's Brigade Wk. EH3	7	M15
Brae Pk. EH4	8	E18
Braeburn Dr., Currie EH14	38	E10
Braefoot Ter. EH16	33	O13
Braehead Av. EH4	8	E18
Braehead Bk. EH4	8	E18
Braehead Cres. EH4	8	E18
Braehead Dr. EH4	8	E18
Braehead Gro. EH4	8	E18
Braehead Ln. EH4	8	E18
Braehead Pk. EH4	8	E18
Braehead Rd. EH4	8	E18
Braehead Row EH4	8	E18
Braehead Av.		
Braehead Vw. EH4	8	E18
Braepark Rd. EH4	8	E18
Braeside Rd., Loanh. EH20	48	P8
Braid Av. EH10	31	L13
Braid Cres. EH10	31	L13
Braid Fm. Rd. EH10	31	L13
Braid Hills App. EH10	41	L12
Braid Hills Av. EH10	31	L13
Braid Hills Cres. EH10	41	L12
Braid Hills Dr. EH10	32	M13
Braid Hills Dr. EH16	42	N12
Braid Hills Rd. EH10	41	L12
Braid Mt. EH10	41	L12
Braid Mt. Crest EH10	41	L12
Braid Mt. Ri. EH10	41	L12
Braid Mt. Vw. EH10	41	L12
Braid Rd. EH10	31	L13
Braidburn Cres. EH10	31	L13
Braidburn Ter. EH10	31	L13
Bramble Dr. EH4	16	E17
Bramdean Gro. EH10	41	L12
Bramdean Pl. EH10	41	L12
Bramdean Ri. EH10	41	L12
Bramdean Vw. EH10	41	L12
Brand Dr. EH15	23	R15
Brand Gdns. EH15	23	S16
Brand Pl. EH8	7	N16
Abbeyhill		
Brandfield St. EH3	6	L15
Brandon St. EH3	20	M17
Brandon Ter. EH3	20	M17
Bread St. EH3	6	L16
Bread St. La. EH3	6	L16
Breadalbane St. EH6	12	N19
Breadalbane Ter. EH11	19	L16
Brewery La. EH6	12	N19
Great Junct. St.		
Briarbank Ter. EH11	30	K14
Brickfield EH15	22	R17
Pipe St.		
Brickwork Clo. EH6	12	N19
Giles St.		
Bridge End EH16	33	O14
Bridge Pl. EH3	19	L17
Bridge Rd. EH13	39	H11
Bridge Rd., Bal. EH14	45	C9
Bridge St. EH15	22	R17
Bridge St., Muss. EH21	25	V15
Bridge St. La. EH15	22	R17
Bridgend, Dalk. EH22	50	T10
Bridgend Ct., Dalk. EH22	50	T10
Briery Bauks EH8	7	N16
Bright Ter. EH11	19	L16
Brighton Pl. EH15	22	R16
Brighton St. EH1	7	M16
Bright's Cres. EH9	32	N14
Bristo Pl. EH1	7	M16
Bristo Port EH1	7	M16
Bristo Sq. EH8	7	M16
Britwell Cres. EH7	22	P17
Broad Wynd EH6	12	O19
Broombank Ter. EH12	29	F14
Broomburn Gro. EH12	29	G15
Broomfield Cres. EH12	29	G14
Broomhall Av. EH12	29	F14
Broomhall Bk. EH12	28	F15
Broomhall Cres. EH12	28	F15
Broomhall Dr. EH12	28	F15
Broomhall Gdns. EH12	28	F15
Broomhall Ln. EH12	28	F15
Broomhall Pk. EH12	28	F15
Broomhall Pl. EH12	28	F15
Broomhall Rd. EH12	28	F15
Broomhall Ter. EH12	28	F15
Broomhill Dr., Dalk. EH22	49	T9
Broomhill Pk., Dalk. EH22	49	T9
Broomhouse Av. EH11	29	F14
Broomhouse Bk. EH11	29	G14
Broomhouse Cotts. EH11	29	G14
Broomhouse Cotts. E. EH11	29	G14
Broomhouse Ct. EH11	29	G14
Broomhouse Cres. EH11	29	F14
Broomhouse Dr. EH11	29	F14
Broomhouse Gdns. EH11	29	F14
Broomhouse Gdns. E. EH11	29	G14
Broomhouse Gdns. W. EH11	29	F14
Broomhouse Gro. EH11	29	G14
Broomhouse Ln. EH11	29	G14
Broomhouse Mkt. EH11	29	G14
Broomhouse Medway EH11	29	G14
Broomhouse Pk. EH11	29	F14
Broomhouse Path EH11	29	F14
Broomhouse Pl. N. EH11	29	F14
Broomhouse Pl. S. EH11	29	G14
Broomhouse Rd. EH11	28	F14
Broomhouse Rd. EH12	28	F14
Broomhouse Row EH11	29	G14
Broomhouse Sq. EH11	29	G14
Broomhouse St. N. EH11	29	F14
Broomhouse St. S. EH11	29	G13
Broomhouse Ter. EH11	29	G14
Broomhouse Wk. EH11	29	G14
Broomhouse Way EH11	29	G14
Broomhouse Wynd EH11	29	G14
Broomieknowe, Lass. EH18	49	R8
Broomieknowe Gdns.,	49	R8
Bonny. EH19		
Broomieknowe Pk., Bonny.	49	R8
EH19		
Broomlea Cres. EH12	29	F15
Broompark Rd. EH12	29	F15
Broomside Ter. EH12	29	G15
Broomview Ho. EH11	29	F13
Broomyknowe EH14	40	H12
Brougham Pl. EH3	6	M15
Brougham St. EH3	6	M15
Broughton Mkt. EH3	7	M17
Broughton Pl. EH1	7	M17
Broughton Pl. La. EH1	20	M17
Broughton Pl.		
Broughton Rd. EH7	12	M18
Broughton St. EH1	7	M17
Broughton St. La. EH1	7	M17
Brown St. EH8	7	N16
Brown St. La. EH8	7	N16
Brown St.		
Brown's Clo. EH8	7	N16
Canongate		
Brown's Pl. EH1	6	M16
Vennel		
Bruce Gdns., Dalk. EH22	50	U9
Bruce St. EH10	31	L13
Brunstane Bk. EH15	23	S15
Brunstane Cres. EH15	23	S15
Brunstane Dr. EH15	23	S15
Brunstane Gdns. EH15	23	S16
Brunstane Gdns. Ms. EH15	23	S16
Brunstane Gdns.		
Brunstane Rd. EH15	23	S16
Brunstane Rd. N. EH15	23	S16
Brunstane Rd. S. EH15	23	S15
Brunstanegate EH15	23	S15
Brunston's Clo. EH1	7	M16
High St.		
Brunswick Pl. EH7	20	N17
Brunswick Rd. EH7	20	N17
Brunswick St. EH7	7	N17
Brunswick St. La. EH7	20	N17
Brunswick Ter. EH7	20	N17
Brunswick Rd.		
Brunton Gdns. EH7	20	N17
Montgomery St.		
Brunton Pl. EH7	7	N17
Brunton Ter. EH7	7	N17
Brunton's Clo., Dalk. EH22	50	U10
Bruntsfield Av. EH10	31	L15
Bruntsfield Cres. EH10	31	L15
Bruntsfield Gdns. EH10	31	L15
Bruntsfield Pl. EH10	31	L14
Bruntsfield Ter. EH10	31	L15
Bryce Av. EH7	22	Q17
Bryce Cres., Currie EH14	38	E11
Bryce Gdns., Currie EH14	38	E11
Bryce Rd.		
Bryce Gro. EH7	22	Q17
Bryce Pl., Currie EH14	38	E11
Bryce Rd., Currie EH14	38	E11
Bryson Rd. EH11	31	K15
Buccleuch Pl. EH8	7	M15
Buccleuch St. EH8	7	N15
Buccleuch St., Dalk. EH22	50	U10
Buccleuch Ter. EH8	20	N15
Buchanan St. EH6	12	N18
Buckingham Ter. EH4	19	K17

Name		
Buckstane Pk. EH10	41	L12
Buckstone Av. EH10	41	L11
Buckstone Bk. EH10	41	L12
Buckstone Circle EH10	41	M11
Buckstone Clo. EH10	41	M11
Buckstone Ct. EH10	41	L11
Buckstone Cres. EH10	41	L12
Buckstone Crook EH10	41	M11
Buckstone Dell EH10	41	L12
Buckstone Dr. EH10	41	L12
Buckstone Gdns. EH10	41	L11
Buckstone Gate EH10	41	M11
Buckstone Grn. EH10	41	L11
Buckstone Gro. EH10	41	L12
Buckstone Hill EH10	41	L12
Buckstone Howe EH10	41	M11
Buckstone Lea EH10	41	M11
Buckstone Ln. EH10	41	L11
Buckstone Ln. E. EH10	41	M11
Buckstone Neuk EH10	41	M11
Buckstone Pl. EH10	41	L11
Buckstone Ri. EH10	41	M11
Buckstone Rd. EH10	41	L11
Buckstone Row EH10	41	M12
Buckstone Shaw EH10	41	M11
Buckstone Ter. EH10	41	L11
Buckstone Vw. EH10	41	L12
Buckstone Way EH10	41	L12
Buckstone Wd. EH10	41	L11
Buckstone Wynd EH10	41	M11
Buckstoneside EH10	41	M11
Buckstone Circle		
Bughtlin Dr. EH12	16	E17
Bughtlin Gdns. EH12	16	E16
Bughtlin Grn. EH12	16	E17
Bughtlin Ln. EH12	16	E16
Bughtlin Mkt. EH12	16	E17
Bughtlin Pk. EH12	16	E16
Bughtlin Pl. EH12	16	E17
Bull's Clo. EH8	7	N16
Burdiehouse Av. EH17	42	O10
Burdiehouse Cres. EH17	43	O10
Burdiehouse Crossway EH17	42	O10
Burdiehouse Dr. EH17	42	O10
Burdiehouse Ln. EH17	42	O10
Burdiehouse Medway EH17	42	O10
Burdiehouse Pl. EH17	42	O10
Burdiehouse Rd. EH17	42	O10
Burdiehouse Sq. EH17	42	O10
Burdiehouse St. EH17	42	O10
Burdiehouse Ter. EH17	42	O10
Burgess St. EH6	12	O19
Burgess Ter. EH9	33	O14
Burghlee Cres., Loanh. EH20	47	O8
Burghlee Ter., Loanh. EH20	47	P8
Burghtoft EH17	43	Q11
Burlington St. EH6	12	N19
Burnbank, Loanh. EH20	47	O8
Burnbank Cres., Loanh. EH20	47	O9
Burnbank Gro., Loanh. EH20	47	O9
Burnbrae EH12	16	E16
Burndene Dr. (Strait.), Loanh. EH20	47	N9
Burnhead Cres. EH16	42	O12
Burnhead Gro. EH16	42	O11
Burnhead Ln. EH16	42	O11
Burnhead Path E. EH16	42	O11
Burnhead Path W. EH16	42	O11
Burns St. EH6	12	O18
Burnside EH12	16	E16
Burnside Pk., Bal. EH14	44	B9
Bush St., Muss. EH21	24	U16
Bush Ter., Muss. EH21	24	U15
Cables Wynd EH6	12	N19
Caddell's Row EH4	8	E19
Cadiz St. EH6	12	O19
Cadogan Rd. EH16	42	O12
Cadzow Pl. EH7	21	O17
Caerketton Cotts. EH13	40	K12
Caerketton Ct. EH13	40	K12
Caerlaverock Ct. EH12	16	E16
Craigievar Wynd		
Cairds Row, Muss. EH21	24	U16
Cairnmuir Rd. EH12	17	G16
Cairns Dr., Bal. EH14	44	B8
Cairns Gdns., Bal. EH14	44	B8
Cairntows Clo. EH16	33	P14
Caithness Pl. EH5	11	L19
Caiy Stane EH10	41	L11
Caiyside EH10	41	L10
Caiystane Av. EH10	41	L11
Caiystane Cres. EH10	41	L11
Caiystane Dr. EH10	41	K11
Caiystane Gdns. EH10	41	K11
Caiystane Hill EH10	41	L11
Caiystane Ter. EH10	41	K11
Caiystane Vw. EH10	41	L11
Calder Ct. EH11	28	F13
Calder Cres. EH11	28	E13
Calder Dr. EH11	28	F13
Calder Gdns. EH11	28	E13
Calder Gro. EH11	28	F13
Calder Pk. EH11	28	F13
Calder Pl. EH11	28	F13
Calder Rd. EH11	29	G13
Calder Rd. Gdns. EH11	29	H14
Calder Vw. EH11	28	E13
Caledonian Cres. EH11	19	K15
Caledonian Pl. EH11	19	K15
Caledonian Rd. EH11	19	L15
Calton Hill EH1	7	N17
Calton Hill EH7	7	N17
Calton Rd. EH8	7	M16
Cambridge Av. EH6	12	N18
Cambridge Gdns. EH6	12	N18
Cambridge St. EH1	6	L16
Cambridge St. La. EH1	6	L16
Cambusnethan St. EH7	21	O17
Cameron Cres. EH16	33	O14
Cameron Ho. Av. EH16	33	O14
Cameron March EH16	33	O14
Cameron Pk. EH16	33	O14
Cameron Smail Rd. (Ricc.), Currie EH14	37	D12
Cameron Ter. EH16	33	O14
Cameron Toll EH16	33	O14
Cameron Toll Gdns. EH16	33	O14
Cammo Bk. EH4	16	E17
Cammo Brae EH4	16	E17
Cammo Cres. EH4	16	E17
Cammo Gdns. EH4	16	E17
Cammo Gro. EH4	15	D17
Cammo Hill EH4	15	D17
Cammo Parkway EH4	16	E17
Cammo Pl. EH4	16	E17
Cammo Rd. EH4	15	D17
Cammo Rd. EH12	15	C17
Cammo Wk. EH4	15	D17
Campbell Av. EH12	18	J16
Campbell Pk. Cres. EH13	39	G11
Campbell Pk. Dr. EH13	39	G11
Campbell Rd. EH12	18	J16
Campbell's Clo. EH8	7	N16
Calton Rd.		
Campie Ct., Muss. EH21	24	U15
Campie Gdns.		
Campie Gdns., Muss. EH21	24	U15
Campie La., Muss. EH21	24	U15
Campie Rd., Muss. EH21	24	U15
Campview (Dand.), Dalk. EH22	51	R12
Campview Av. (Dand.), Dalk. EH22	51	R12
Campview Cres. (Dand.), Dalk. EH22	51	R12
Campview Gdns. (Dand.), Dalk. EH22	51	R12
Campview Gro. (Dand.), Dalk. EH22	51	S12
Campview Ter. (Dand.), Dalk. EH22	51	R12
Camus Av. EH10	41	L11
Camus Pk. EH10	41	L11
Camus Pl. E. EH10	41	L11
Camus Rd. E. EH10	41	L11
Camus Rd. W. EH10	41	L11
Canaan La. EH10	31	L14
Candlemaker Row EH1	7	M16
Candlemaker's Cres. EH17	43	Q11
Candlemaker's Pk. EH17	43	Q11
Canning St. EH3	6	L16
Canning St. La. EH3	6	L16
Cannon Wynd EH6	12	N19
Canon La. EH3	20	M17
Canon St. EH3	20	M17
Canongate EH8	7	N16
Canonmills EH3	11	M18
Capelaw Ct. EH13	40	K12
Capelaw Rd. EH13	39	H11
Captain's Dr. EH16	42	O11
Captain's Ln. EH16	42	O11
Captain's Rd. EH17	42	O11
Captain's Row EH16	42	O11
Carberry Pl. EH12	18	K16
Carberry Rd. (Inver.), Muss. EH21	25	V14
Carfrae Gdns. EH4	17	H17
Carfrae Gro. EH4	17	H17
Carfrae Pk. EH4	17	H17
Carfrae Rd. EH4	17	H17
Cargil Ct. EH5	11	L19
Cargil Ter. EH5	11	L19
Carlton St. EH4	6	L17
Carlton Ter. EH7	7	N17
Carlton Ter. Brae EH7	7	N17
Carlton Ter. La. EH7	7	N17
Carlton Ter. Ms. EH7	7	N17
Carlyle Pl. EH7	21	O17
Carlyle Pl., Muss. EH21	24	V15
Carnbee Av. EH16	43	P11
Carnbee Cres. EH16	43	P11
Carnbee Dell EH16	43	P11
Carnbee End EH16	43	P11
Carnbee Pk. EH16	43	P11
Carnegie Ct. EH8	7	N16
Carnegie St. EH8	7	N16
Carnethy Av. EH13	39	H11
Caroline Gdns. EH12	17	G16
Caroline Pk. Av. EH5	10	J20
Caroline Pk. Gro. EH5	10	J19
Caroline Pl. EH12	17	G16
Caroline Ter. EH12	16	F16
Carpet La. EH6	12	O19
Bernard St.		
Carrick Cres. (Easth.), Dalk. EH22	50	V8
Carrick Knowe Av. EH12	29	G15
Carrick Knowe Dr. EH12	29	G15
Carrick Knowe Gdns. EH12	29	G15
Carrick Knowe Gro. EH12	29	G15
Carrick Knowe Hill EH12	29	G15
Carrick Knowe Ln. EH12	29	G15
Carrick Knowe Parkway EH12	29	G15
Carrick Knowe Pl. EH12	29	G15
Carrick Knowe Rd. EH12	29	G14
Carrick Knowe Ter. EH12	29	G15
Carrington Cres. EH4	10	K18
Crewe Rd. S.		
Carrington Rd. EH4	19	K17
Carron Pl. EH6	13	O19
Carrubber's Clo. EH1	7	M16
High St.		
Casselbank St. EH6	12	N18
Cassel's La. EH6	12	N18
Castle Av. EH12	29	F15
Castle Esp. EH1	6	M16
Castle St. EH2	6	L16
Castle Ter. EH1	6	L16
Castle Ter. EH3	6	L16
Castle Wynd N. EH1	20	M16
Castle Wynd S. EH1	20	M16
Johnston Ter.		
Castlehill EH1	6	M16
Castlelaw Rd. EH13	39	H11
Castleview Ho. EH17	33	P13
Cathcart Pl. EH11	19	K15
Cathedral La. EH1	7	M17
Catherine Pl. EH3	11	M18
Cattle Rd. EH14	30	H14
Causeway, The EH15	21	P15
Causewayside EH9	32	N15
Cavalry Pk. Dr. EH15	22	P15
Cedars, The EH13	40	H12
Cemetery Rd., Dalk. EH22	50	T10
Chalmers Bldgs. EH3	6	L15
Fountainbridge		
Chalmers Clo. EH1	7	M16
High St.		
Chalmers Cres. EH9	32	M15
Chalmers St. EH3	6	M15
Chamberlain Rd. EH10	31	L14
Chambers St. EH1	7	M16
Champigny Ct., Muss. EH21	25	W15
Chancelot Cres. EH6	11	M19
Chancelot Gro. EH5	11	M19
Chancelot Ter. EH6	11	M19
Chapel Ct. EH16	34	Q14
Chapel La. EH6	12	O19
Maritime St.		
Chapel St. EH8	7	N15

Name	Page	Ref
Chapel Wynd EH1	6	M16
West Port		
Charles St. EH8	7	M16
Charles St. La. EH8	7	M16
Charlesfield EH8	7	M16
Bristo Sq.		
Charlotte La. EH2	6	L16
Charlotte Sq. EH2	6	L16
Charterhall Gro. EH9	32	M14
Charterhall Rd. EH9	32	M13
Chatterrig EH13	40	K12
Cherry Tree Av., Bal. EH14	45	D10
Cherry Tree Cres., Bal. EH14	45	C10
Cherry Tree Cres., Currie EH14	45	C10
Cherry Tree Gdns., Bal. EH14	45	C10
Cherry Tree Gro., Bal. EH14	45	C10
Cherry Tree Ln., Bal. EH14	45	D10
Cherry Tree Pk., Bal. EH14	45	C10
Cherry Tree Pl., Currie EH14	45	D10
Cherry Tree Vw., Bal. EH14	45	D10
Chessels Ct. EH8	7	N16
Chesser Av. EH14	30	H14
Chesser Cotts. EH11	30	H14
Gorgie Rd.		
Chesser Cres. EH14	30	J14
Chesser Gdns. EH14	30	H14
Chesser Gro. EH14	30	H14
Chesser Ln. EH14	30	H14
Chester St. EH3	19	L16
Chestnut St. EH5	10	K20
Cheyne St. EH4	19	L17
Christian Cres. EH15	23	R16
Christian Gro. EH15	23	R16
Christian Path EH15	22	R16
Christiemiller Av. EH7	22	Q17
Christiemiller Gro. EH7	22	Q17
Christiemiller Pl. EH7	22	Q17
Chuckie Pend EH3	6	L16
Church Hill EH10	31	L14
Church Hill Dr. EH10	31	L14
Church Hill Pl. EH10	31	L14
Church La., Muss. EH21	25	V15
Church Rd., Lass. EH18	48	Q9
Church St., Loanh. EH20	48	P8
Circle, The	51	R12
(Dand.), Dalk. EH22		
Circus Gdns. EH3	6	L17
Circus La. EH3	6	L17
Citadel Ct. EH6	12	N19
Citadel Pl. EH6	12	N19
Commercial St.		
Citadel St. EH6	12	N19
City of Edinburgh Bypass, The EH10	40	J11
City of Edinburgh Bypass, The EH12	27	D15
City of Edinburgh Bypass, The EH13	40	J11
City of Edinburgh Bypass, The EH14	38	F12
City of Edinburgh Bypass, The EH17	46	N10
City of Edinburgh Bypass, The, Lass. EH18	48	Q10
Clackmae Gro. EH16	42	N12
Clackmae Rd. EH16	42	N12
Clapper La. EH16	33	O13
Clapperton Pl. EH7	21	O17
Lower London Rd.		
Clarebank Cres. EH6	13	O18
Claremont Bk. EH7	20	M17
Claremont Ct. EH7	12	M18
Claremont Cres. EH7	12	M18
Claremont Gdns. EH6	13	O18
Claremont Gro. EH7	12	M18
Claremont Pk. EH6	13	O18
Claremont Rd. EH6	13	O18
Clarence St. EH3	19	L17
Clarendon Cres. EH4	6	L17
Clarinda Gdns., Dalk. EH22	50	V9
Clarinda Ter. EH16	33	O13
Clark Av. EH5	11	M19
Clark Pl. EH5	11	L19
Clark Rd. EH5	11	L19
Claverhouse Dr. EH16	42	O12
Clayhills Gro., Bal. EH14	44	B9
Clayhills Pk., Bal. EH14	44	B9
Clayknowes Av., Muss. EH21	24	U15
Clayknowes Ct., Muss. EH21	24	U14
Clayknowes Dr., Muss. EH21	24	T15
Clayknowes Pl., Muss. EH21	24	T15
Clayknowes Rd., Muss. EH21	24	U15
Clayknowes Way, Muss. EH21	24	U15
Clearburn Cres. EH16	33	O14
Clearburn Gdns. EH16	33	O14
Clearburn Rd. EH16	33	O14
Cleekim Dr. EH15	34	R14
Cleekim Rd. EH15	34	R14
Cleikiminfield EH15	35	R14
Cleikiminrig EH15	35	R14
Clerk St. EH8	20	N15
Clerk St., Loanh. EH20	47	P8
Clermiston Av. EH4	16	F17
Clermiston Cres. EH4	17	F17
Clermiston Dr. EH4	16	F17
Clermiston Gdns. EH4	17	F17
Clermiston Grn. EH4	16	F17
Clermiston Gro. EH4	17	F17
Clermiston Hill EH4	17	F17
Clermiston Ln. EH4	16	F17
Clermiston Medway EH4	17	F17
Clermiston Pk. EH4	17	F17
Clermiston Pl. EH4	17	F17
Clermiston Rd. EH12	17	G16
Clermiston Rd. N. EH4	17	G17
Clermiston Ter. EH12	17	G16
Clermiston Vw. EH4	17	G17
Clerwood Bk. EH12	16	F16
Clerwood Gdns. EH12	16	F16
Clerwood Gro. EH12	17	G16
Clerwood Ln. EH12	16	F16
Clerwood Pk. EH12	17	F16
Clerwood Pl. EH12	17	G16
Clerwood Row EH12	16	F16
Clerwood Ter. EH12	17	G16
Clerwood Vw. EH12	17	G16
Clerwood Way EH12	16	F16
Clifton Sq. EH15	22	R16
Baileyfield Rd.		
Clifton Ter. EH12	19	L16
Clinton Rd. EH9	31	L14
Clockmill La. EH8	21	O17
Clovenstone Dr. EH14	39	G12
Clovenstone Gdns. EH14	39	G12
Clovenstone Pk. EH14	39	G12
Clovenstone Rd. EH14	39	G12
Cluny Av. EH10	31	L13
Cluny Dr. EH10	31	L13
Cluny Gdns. EH10	31	L13
Cluny Pl. EH10	32	M13
Cluny Ter. EH10	31	L13
Clyde St. EH1	20	M17
Coalhill EH6	12	N19
Coates Cres. EH3	6	L16
Coates Gdns. EH12	19	K16
Coates Pl. EH3	19	L16
Coatfield La. EH6	12	O19
Cobbinshaw Ho. EH11	28	F13
Cobden Cres. EH9	32	N14
Cobden Rd. EH9	32	N14
Cobden Ter. EH11	19	L16
Coburg St. EH6	12	N19
Cochran Pl. EH7	20	M17
East London St.		
Cochran Ter. EH7	20	M17
Cochrane Pl. EH6	12	O18
Cockburn Cres., Bal. EH14	44	B8
Cockburn St. EH1	7	M16
Cockburnhill Rd., Bal. EH14	44	B8
Cockmylane EH10	41	K11
Coffin La. EH11	19	K15
Coillesdene Av. EH15	23	S16
Coillesdene Cres. EH15	23	S16
Coillesdene Dr. EH15	23	S16
Coillesdene Gdns. EH15	23	S16
Coillesdene Gro. EH15	23	S16
Coillesdene Ln. EH15	24	T16
Coillesdene Ter. EH15	23	S16
Coinyie Ho. Clo. EH1	7	N16
Blackfriars St.		
Colinton Gro. EH14	30	J13
Colinton Gro. W. EH14	30	J13
Colinton Mains Cres. EH13	40	J11
Colinton Mains Dr. EH13	40	J12
Colinton Mains Gdns. EH13	40	J12
Colinton Mains Grn. EH13	40	J12
Colinton Mains Gro. EH13	40	K12
Colinton Mains Ln. EH13	40	J12
Colinton Mains Pl. EH13	40	K12
Colinton Mains Rd. EH13	40	J12
Colinton Mains Ter. EH13	40	K12
Colinton Rd. EH10	31	K14
Colinton Rd. EH13	40	H12
Colinton Rd. EH14	30	J13
College Wynd EH1	7	M16
Cowgate		
Collins Pl. EH3	19	L17
Colmestone Gate EH10	41	L11
Coltbridge Av. EH12	18	J16
Coltbridge Gdns. EH12	18	K16
Coltbridge Millside EH12	18	J16
Coltbridge Av.		
Coltbridge Ter. EH12	18	J16
Coltbridge Vale EH12	18	K16
Columba Av. EH4	18	H17
Columba Rd. EH4	18	H17
Colville Pl. EH3	19	L17
Comely Bk. EH4	19	K17
Comely Bk. Av. EH4	19	L17
Comely Bk. Gro. EH4	19	K17
Comely Bk. Pl. EH4	19	L17
Comely Bk. Pl. Ms. EH4	19	L17
Comely Bk. Rd. EH4	19	K17
Comely Bk. Row EH4	19	L17
Comely Bk. St. EH4	19	K17
Comely Bk. Ter. EH4	19	L17
Comely Grn. Cres. EH7	21	O17
Comely Grn. Pl. EH7	21	O17
Comiston Dr. EH10	31	K13
Comiston Gdns. EH10	31	L13
Comiston Gro. EH10	41	L12
Comiston Pl. EH10	31	L13
Comiston Ri. EH10	41	L12
Comiston Rd. EH10	41	L12
Comiston Springs Av. EH10	41	L12
Comiston Ter. EH10	31	L13
Comiston Vw. EH10	41	L12
Commercial St. EH6	12	N19
Commercial Wf. EH6	12	O19
Connaught Pl. EH6	12	M19
Considine Gdns. EH8	21	P17
Considine Ter. EH8	21	P17
Constitution Pl. EH6	12	O19
Constitution St. EH6	12	O18
Convening Ct. EH4	19	K17
Dean Path		
Corbiehill Av. EH4	9	H18
Corbiehill Cres. EH4	9	G18
Corbiehill Gdns. EH4	9	H18
Corbiehill Gro. EH4	9	H18
Corbiehill Pk. EH4	9	G18
Corbiehill Pl. EH4	9	G18
Corbiehill Rd. EH4	9	G18
Corbiehill Ter. EH4	9	G18
Corbieshot EH15	35	R15
Cornhill Ter. EH6	13	O18
Cornwall St. EH1	6	L16
Cornwallis Pl. EH3	20	M17
Coronation Wk. EH3	20	M15
Corporation Bldgs. EH6	12	N19
Sheriff Brae		
Corrennie Dr. EH10	31	L13
Corrennie Gdns. EH10	31	L13
Corslet Cres., Currie EH14	38	E11
Corslet Pl., Currie EH14	38	E11
Corslet Rd., Currie EH14	38	E11
Corstorphine Bk. Av. EH12	16	F16
Corstorphine Bk. Dr. EH12	16	F16
Corstorphine Bk. Ter. EH12	16	F16
Corstorphine High St. EH12	16	F15
Corstorphine Hill Av. EH12	17	G16
Corstorphine Hill Cres. EH12	17	G16
Corstorphine Hill Gdns. EH12	17	G16
Corstorphine Hill Rd. EH12	17	G16
Corstorphine Ho. Av. EH12	17	G15
Corstorphine Ho. Ter. EH12	17	G15
Corstorphine Pk. Gdns. EH12	17	G15
Corstorphine Rd. EH12	17	H15
Cortleferry Dr., Dalk. EH22	49	T9
Cortleferry Gro., Dalk. EH22	49	T9
Cortleferry Pk., Dalk. EH22	49	T9
Cortleferry Ter., Dalk. EH22	49	T9
Corunna Pl. EH6	12	N19
Cottage Grn. EH4	8	E18
Cottage Homes EH13	40	H11
Cottage La., Muss. EH21	25	W15
Cottage Pk. EH4	17	H17
Couper St. EH6	12	N19
Cowan Rd. EH11	30	K14
Cowan's Clo. EH8	7	N15
Cowden Cres., Dalk. EH22	50	V10
Cowden Gro., Dalk. EH22	50	V10

Name	Page	Grid
Cowden La., Dalk. EH22	50	V10
Cowden Pk., Dalk. EH22	50	V10
Cowden Ter., Dalk. EH22	50	V10
Cowden Vw., Dalk. EH22	50	V10
Cowgate EH1	7	M16
Cowgatehead EH1	20	M16
Cowpits (White.), Muss. EH21	25	V13
Cowpits Rd.	25	V13
(White.), Muss. EH21		
Coxfield EH11	30	J14
Craigcrook Av. EH4	17	H17
Craigcrook Gdns. EH4	18	H17
Craigcrook Gro. EH4	17	H17
Craigcrook Pk. EH4	17	H17
Craigcrook Pl. EH4	18	H17
Craigcrook Rd. EH4	17	G17
Craigcrook Sq. EH4	17	H17
Craigcrook Ter. EH4	18	H17
Craigend Pk. EH16	33	P13
Craigentinny Av. EH7	22	Q17
Craigentinny Av. N. EH6	13	P18
Craigentinny Cres. EH7	22	Q17
Craigentinny Gro. EH7	22	Q17
Craigentinny Pl. EH7	22	Q17
Craigentinny Rd. EH7	22	P17
Craighall Av. EH6	11	M19
Craighall Bk. EH6	11	M19
Craighall Cres. EH6	11	M19
Craighall Gdns. EH6	11	M19
Craighall Rd. EH6	11	M19
Craighall Ter. EH6	11	M19
Craighall Ter., Muss. EH21	25	W15
Craighill Gdns. EH10	31	K13
Craighouse Av. EH10	31	K13
Craighouse Gdns. EH10	31	K13
Craighouse Pk. EH10	31	K13
Craighouse Rd. EH10	31	K13
Craighouse Ter. EH10	31	K13
Craigievar Ct. EH12	16	E16
Craigievar Wynd		
Craigievar Sq. EH12	16	E16
Craigievar Wynd EH12	16	E16
Craiglea Dr. EH10	31	K13
Craiglea Pl. EH10	31	K13
Craigleith Av. N. EH4	18	J16
Craigleith Av. S. EH4	18	J16
Craigleith Bk. EH4	18	J17
Craigleith Cres. EH4	18	J17
Craigleith Dr. EH4	18	J17
Craigleith Gdns. EH4	18	J17
Craigleith Gro. EH4	18	J17
Craigleith Hill EH4	18	J17
Craigleith Hill Av. EH4	18	J17
Craigleith Hill Cres. EH4	18	J17
Craigleith Hill Gdns. EH4	18	J17
Craigleith Hill Grn. EH4	18	J17
Craigleith Hill Gro. EH4	18	J17
Craigleith Hill Ln. EH4	18	J17
Craigleith Hill Pk. EH4	18	J17
Craigleith Hill Row EH4	18	J17
Craigleith Ri. EH4	18	J16
Craigleith Rd. EH4	18	J17
Craigleith Vw. EH4	18	J16
Craiglockhart Av. EH14	30	J13
Craiglockhart Bk. EH14	30	J13
Craiglockhart Cres. EH14	30	J13
Craiglockhart Dell Rd. EH14	30	J13
Craiglockhart Dr. N. EH14	30	J13
Craiglockhart Dr. S. EH14	30	J13
Craiglockhart Gdns. EH14	30	J13
Craiglockhart Gro. EH14	40	J12
Craiglockhart Ln. EH14	30	J13
Craiglockhart Pk. EH14	30	J13
Craiglockhart Pl. EH14	30	J13
Craiglockhart Quad. EH14	30	J13
Craiglockhart Rd. EH14	30	J13
Craiglockhart Rd. N. EH14	30	J13
Craiglockhart Ter. EH14	30	K14
Craiglockhart Vw. EH14	30	J13
Craigmillar Castle Av. EH16	34	P14
Craigmillar Castle Gdns. EH16	33	P14
Craigmillar Castle Gro. EH16	34	P14
Craigmillar Castle Ln. EH16	34	Q14
Craigmillar Castle Rd. EH16	34	P14
Craigmillar Castle Ter. EH16	34	P14
Craigmillar Ct. EH16	33	P14
Craigmillar Pk. EH16	33	N14
Craigmount App. EH12	16	F16
Craigmount Av. EH12	16	F16
Craigmount Av. N. EH4	16	E17
Craigmount Av. N. EH12	16	E17
Craigmount Bk. EH4	16	E17
Craigmount Bk. W. EH4	16	E17
Craigmount Brae EH12	16	E17
Craigmount Ct. EH4	16	E17
Craigmount Cres. EH12	16	E16
Craigmount Dr. EH12	16	E16
Craigmount Gdns. EH12	16	E16
Craigmount Gro. EH12	16	E16
Craigmount Gro. N. EH12	16	E16
Craigmount Hill EH4	16	E17
Craigmount Ln. EH12	16	E16
Craigmount Pk. EH12	16	E16
Craigmount Pl. EH12	16	E16
Craigmount Ter. EH12	16	E16
Craigmount Vw. EH12	16	E16
Craigmount Way EH12	16	F17
Craigour Av. EH17	43	Q12
Craigour Cres. EH17	43	Q12
Craigour Dr. EH17	43	Q12
Craigour Gdns. EH17	43	Q12
Craigour Grn. EH17	43	P12
Craigour Gro. EH17	43	Q12
Craigour Ln. EH17	43	Q12
Craigour Pl. EH17	43	P12
Craigour Ter. EH17	43	Q12
Craigs Av. EH12	16	E15
Craigs Bk. EH12	16	E16
Craigs Cres. EH12	16	E16
Craigs Dr. EH12	16	E16
Craigs Gdns. EH12	16	E16
Craigs Gro. EH12	16	F16
Craigs Ln. EH12	16	F16
Craigs Pk. EH12	16	E16
Craigs Rd. EH12	16	E16
Crame Ter., Dalk. EH22	49	T9
Cramond Av. EH4	8	E19
Cramond Bk. EH4	8	E19
Cramond Bri. EH4	8	D18
Cramond Bri. Cotts. EH4	8	D18
Queensferry Rd.		
Cramond Brig Toll EH4	8	D18
Cramond Cres. EH4	8	E19
Cramond Gdns. EH4	8	E19
Cramond Glebe Gdns. EH4	8	F19
Cramond Glebe Rd. EH4	8	E20
Cramond Glebe Ter. EH4	8	E19
Cramond Grn. EH4	8	E19
Cramond Gro. EH4	8	E19
Cramond Pk. EH4	8	E19
Cramond Pl. EH4	8	F19
Cramond Regis EH4	8	E18
Cramond Rd. N. EH4	9	F19
Cramond Rd. S. EH4	8	E19
Cramond Ter. EH4	8	E19
Cramond Vale EH4	8	E19
Cramond Village EH4	8	E20
Cranston St. EH8	7	N16
Crarae Av. EH4	18	J16
Craufurdland EH4	8	E18
Crawford Bri. EH7	21	O17
Bothwell St.		
Crawfurd Rd. EH16	33	N14
Crescent, The EH10	31	L13
Crescent, The EH11	30	H14
Gorgie Rd.		
Crewe Bk. EH5	10	K19
Crewe Cres. EH5	10	J19
Crewe Gro. EH5	10	K19
Crewe Ln. EH5	10	J19
Crewe Path EH5	10	J19
Crewe Pl. EH5	10	J19
Crewe Rd. Gdns. EH5	10	J19
Crewe Rd. N. EH5	10	K18
Crewe Rd. S. EH4	10	J19
Crewe Rd. W. EH5	10	J19
Crewe Ter. EH5	10	J19
Crewe Toll EH4	10	J18
Crichton St. EH8	7	M16
Crighton Pl. EH7	12	N18
Croall Pl. EH7	20	N17
Croft St., Dalk. EH22	50	U10
Croft-an-righ EH8	21	N17
Cromwell Pl. EH6	12	N19
Crookston Rd.	25	W14
(Inver.), Muss. EH21		
Cross Rd., Loanh. EH20	47	N8
Crosswood Av., Bal. EH14	44	B8
Crosswood Cres., Bal. EH14	44	B8
Crown Pl. EH6	12	N18
Crown St. EH6	12	N18
Cuddy La. EH10	31	L14
Cuguen Pl., Lass. EH18	49	R9
Cultins Rd. EH11	28	E14
Cumberland St. EH3	6	M17
Cumberland St. N. E. La. EH3	20	M17
Cumberland St. N. W. La. EH3	20	M17
Cumberland St. S. E. La. EH3	20	M17
Cumberland St. S. W. La. EH3	6	M17
Cumin Pl. EH9	32	N15
Cumlodden Av. EH12	18	J16
Cumnor Cres. EH16	33	O13
Cunningham Pl. EH6	12	N18
Curriehill Castle Dr., Bal. EH14	45	C10
Curriehill Rd., Currie EH14	37	C12
Currievale Dr., Currie EH14	37	D10
Currievale Pk., Currie EH14	37	D10
Currievale Pk. Gro., Currie EH14	37	D10
Daiches Braes EH15	23	S15
Dairsie Pl. EH7	21	O17
Stanley Pl.		
Daisy Ter. EH11	30	K15
Merchiston Gro.		
Dalgety Av. EH7	21	O17
Dalgety Rd. EH7	21	O17
Dalgety St. EH7	21	O17
Dalhousie Rd., Dalk. EH22	50	T9
Dalhousie Ter. EH10	31	L13
Dalkeith Rd. EH16	32	N15
Dalkeith St. EH15	23	S16
Dalkeith Western Bypass, Dalk. EH22	49	S10
Dalkeith Western Bypass, Lass. EH18	49	S10
Dalmahoy Cres., Bal. EH14	44	B10
Dalmahoy Rd. (Ratho), Newbr. EH28	26	A13
Dalmeny Rd. EH6	12	M19
Dalmeny St. EH6	12	N18
Dalry Pl. EH11	19	L16
Dalry Rd. EH11	19	K15
Dalry Rd. La. EH11	19	K15
Dalry Rd.		
Dalrymple Cres. EH9	32	N14
Dalrymple Cres., Muss. EH21	24	U15
Dalrymple Ln., Muss. EH21	25	V15
Dalum Ct., Loanh. EH20	47	O8
Dalum Dr., Loanh. EH20	47	O8
Dalum Gro., Loanh. EH20	47	O8
Dalum Ln., Loanh. EH20	47	O8
Dalziel Pl. EH7	21	O17
London Rd.		
Damhead EH10	46	M8
Damside EH4	19	K16
Danderhall Cres.	51	R12
(Dand.), Dalk. EH22		
Danube St. EH4	6	L17
Darling's Bldgs. EH3	19	L17
Saunders St.		
Darnaway St. EH3	6	L17
Darnell Rd. EH5	11	L19
Davidson Gdns. EH4	9	H18
Davidson Pk. EH4	10	J18
Davidson Rd. EH4	10	J18
Davie St. EH8	7	N16
Dean Bk. La. EH3	19	L17
Dean Bri. EH3	6	L17
Dean Bri. EH4	6	L17
Dean Pk. Cres. EH4	19	L17
Dean Pk. Ms. EH4	6	L17
Dean Pk. St. EH4	6	L17
Dean Path EH4	19	K17
Dean Path Bldgs. EH4	19	K17
Dean Path		
Dean St. EH4	6	L17
Dean Ter. EH4	6	L17
Deanery Clo. EH7	21	P17
Deanhaugh St. EH4	6	L17
Deanpark Av., Bal. EH14	44	C9
Deanpark Bk., Bal. EH14	45	C9
Deanpark Brae, Bal. EH14	45	C9
Deanpark Ct., Bal. EH14	44	B9
Deanpark Cres., Bal. EH14	45	C9
Deanpark Gdns., Bal. EH14	45	C9
Deanpark Gro., Bal. EH14	45	C9
Deanpark Pl., Bal. EH14	44	C9
Deanpark Sq., Bal. EH14	44	C9
Dechmont Rd. EH12	16	E16
Delhaig EH11	30	J14
Dell Rd. EH13	39	H12
Delta Pl. (Inver.), Muss. EH21	25	V14

Name		
Denham Grn. Av. EH5	11	L19
Denham Grn. Pl. EH5	11	L19
Denham Grn. Ter. EH5	11	L19
Denholm Rd., Muss. EH21	24	T15
Denholm Way, Muss. EH21	24	T14
Derby St. EH6	11	M19
Devon Pl. EH12	19	K16
Dewar Pl. EH3	6	L16
Dewar Pl. La. EH3	6	L16
Dick Pl. EH9	32	M14
Dickson St. EH6	12	N18
Dickson's Clo. EH1	7	M16
High St.		
Dickson's Ct. EH8	7	M16
Bristo Sq.		
Dinmont Dr. EH16	33	O13
Distillery La. EH11	19	L16
Dalry Rd.		
Dobbie's Rd., Bonny. EH19	49	R8
Dobbie's Rd., Lass. EH18	49	R8
Dochart Dr. EH4	16	F17
Dock Pl. EH6	12	N19
Dock St. EH6	12	N19
Dolphin Av., Currie EH14	37	D10
Dolphin Gdns. E., Currie EH14	37	D10
Dolphin Gdns. W., Currie EH14	37	D10
Dolphin Rd., Currie EH14	37	D10
Dorset Pl. EH11	19	L15
Double Dykes	25	V14
(Inver.), Muss. EH21		
Double Hedges Pk. EH16	33	O13
Double Hedges Rd. EH16	33	O13
Douglas Cres. EH12	19	K16
Douglas Cres., Bonny. EH19	49	R8
Douglas Gdns. EH4	19	K16
Douglas Gdns. Ms. EH4	19	K16
Douglas Ter. EH11	19	L16
Doune Ter. EH3	6	L17
Dovecot Gro. EH14	29	H13
Dovecot Ln. EH14	29	H13
Dovecot Pk. EH14	39	H12
Dovecot Rd. EH12	29	F15
Dowie's Mill La. EH4	8	D18
Downfield Pl. EH11	19	K15
Downie Gro. EH12	17	G15
Downie Pl., Muss. EH21	25	V15
Downie Ter. EH12	17	G15
Dreghorn Av. EH13	40	K11
Dreghorn Dr. EH13	40	K11
Dreghorn Gdns. EH13	40	K11
Dreghorn Gro. EH13	40	K11
Dreghorn Link EH13	40	K11
Dreghorn Ln. EH13	39	H11
Dreghorn Pk. EH13	40	J11
Dreghorn Pl. EH13	40	K11
Drum Av. EH17	43	Q11
Drum Brae Av. EH12	16	F16
Drum Brae Cres. EH4	16	F17
Drum Brae Dr. EH4	16	F17
Drum Brae Gdns. EH12	16	F16
Drum Brae Gro. EH4	16	F17
Drum Brae Neuk EH12	16	F16
Drum Brae N. EH4	16	E17
Drum Brae Pk. EH12	16	F16
Drum Brae Pk. App. EH12	16	F16
Drum Brae Pl. EH12	16	F16
Drum Brae S. EH12	16	F16
Drum Brae Ter. EH4	16	F17
Drum Brae Wk. EH4	16	E17
Drum Cotts. EH17	43	Q11
Drum Cres. EH17	43	Q11
Drum Pk. Yd. EH7	21	O17
Albion Rd.		
Drum Pl. EH17	43	Q11
Drum St. EH17	43	Q11
Drum Ter. EH7	21	O17
Drum Vw. Av.	51	R12
(Dand.), Dalk. EH22		
Drumdryan St. EH3	6	L15
Drummond Pl. EH3	6	M17
Drummond St. EH8	7	N16
Drumsheugh Gdns. EH3	6	L16
Drumsheugh Pl. EH3	6	L16
Queensferry St.		
Dryden Av., Loanh. EH20	47	O8
Dryden Cres., Loanh. EH20	47	O8
Dryden Gdns. EH7	12	N18
Dryden Glen, Loanh. EH20	47	N8
Dryden Pl. EH9	32	N15
Dryden Rd., Loanh. EH20	47	N8
Dryden St. EH7	12	N18
Dryden Ter. EH7	12	N18
Dryden Ter., Loanh. EH20	47	O8
Dryden Vw., Loanh. EH20	47	O8
Drylaw Av. EH4	18	J17
Drylaw Cres. EH4	18	H17
Drylaw Gdns. EH4	10	H18
Drylaw Grn. EH4	18	H17
Drylaw Gro. EH4	18	H17
Drylaw Ho. Gdns. EH4	10	H18
Drylaw Ho. Paddock EH4	10	H18
Duart Cres. EH4	16	F17
Dublin Meuse EH3	6	M17
Dublin St. EH1	7	M17
Dublin St. EH3	7	M17
Dublin St. La. EH3	7	M17
Dublin St. La. S. EH1	7	M17
Duddingston Av. EH15	22	Q15
Duddingston Cres. EH15	22	R15
Duddingston Gdns. N. EH15	22	Q15
Duddingston Gdns. S. EH15	22	Q15
Duddingston Gro. E. EH15	22	Q16
Duddingston Gro. W. EH15	22	Q15
Duddingston Ln. EH15	22	Q15
Duddingston Mains Cotts. EH15	22	R15
Milton Rd.		
Duddingston Mills EH8	22	Q16
Duddingston Pk. EH15	22	R16
Duddingston Pk. S. EH15	34	R15
Duddingston Ri. EH15	22	Q15
Duddingston Rd. EH15	22	Q16
Duddingston Rd. W. EH15	22	P15
Duddingston Rd. W. EH16	33	P15
Duddingston Row EH15	22	Q15
Duddingston Sq. E. EH15	22	Q16
Duddingston Sq. W. EH15	22	Q16
Duddingston Vw. EH15	22	Q15
Duddingston Yards EH15	34	R15
Duddingston Pk. S.		
Dudley Av. EH6	12	M19
Dudley Av. S. EH6	12	M19
Dudley Bk. EH6	12	M19
Dudley Cres. EH6	12	M19
Dudley Gdns. EH6	12	M19
Dudley Gro. EH6	12	M19
Dudley Ter. EH6	12	M19
Duff St. EH11	19	K15
Duff St. La. EH11	19	K15
Duke Pl. EH6	12	O18
Duke St. EH6	12	O18
Duke St., Dalk. EH22	50	U10
Duke's Wk. EH8	21	O17
Dumbiedykes Rd. EH8	7	N16
Dumbryden Dr. EH14	29	G13
Dumbryden Gdns. EH14	29	G13
Dumbryden Gro. EH14	29	G13
Dumbryden Rd. EH14	29	G13
Dun-ard Gdn. EH9	32	M14
Dunbar St. EH3	6	L16
Duncan Pl. EH6	12	O18
Duncan St. EH9	32	N14
Duncans Gait EH14	29	G13
Dundas Cres., Dalk. EH22	50	T9
Dundas Gro., Dalk. EH22	50	T9
Dundas Pk., Bonny. EH19	49	S8
Dundas Rd., Dalk. EH22	50	T9
Dundas St. EH3	6	M17
Dundas St., Bonny. EH19	49	R8
Dundee St. EH11	19	K15
Dundee Ter. EH11	19	K15
Dundonald St. EH3	20	M17
Dundrennan Cotts. EH16	33	P13
Dunedin St. EH7	12	M18
Dunlop's Ct. EH1	6	M16
Grassmarket		
Dunollie Ct. EH12	16	E16
Craigievar Wynd		
Dunrobin Pl. EH3	19	L17
Dunsmuir Ct. EH12	16	F15
Dunsyre Ho. EH11	28	F13
Dunvegan Ct. EH4	8	E18
Durar Dr. EH4	16	F17
Durham Av. EH15	22	Q16
Durham Dr. EH15	22	R15
Durham Gdns. N. EH15	22	R16
Durham Gdns. S. EH15	22	R15
Durham Gro. EH15	22	R16
Durham Pl. EH3	20	M17
Dundas St.		
Durham Pl. E. EH15	22	R16
Durham Pl. La. EH15	22	R16
Durham Pl. W. EH15	22	Q15
Durham Rd. EH15	22	R16
Durham Rd. S. EH15	22	R15
Durham Sq. EH15	22	Q16
Durham Ter. EH15	22	Q16
Durward Gro. EH16	33	O13
Earl Grey St. EH3	6	L16
Earl Haig Gdns. EH5	11	L19
Earl Haig Homes EH11	29	H14
Earlston Pl. EH7	21	O17
East Adam St. EH8	7	N16
East Barnton Av. EH4	9	G18
East Barnton Gdns. EH4	9	G18
East Brighton Cres. EH15	22	R16
East Broughton Pl. EH1	20	M17
Broughton Pl.		
East Caistyane Pl. EH10	41	L11
East Caistyane Rd. EH10	41	L11
East Castle Rd. EH10	31	L15
East Champanyie EH9	32	N14
East Clapperfield EH16	33	O13
East Claremont St. EH7	20	M17
East Comiston EH10	41	L11
East Ct. EH4	18	J17
East Ct. EH16	34	Q14
East Cft.	26	A13
(Ratho), Newbr. EH28		
East Cromwell St. EH6	12	N19
East Crosscauseway EH8	7	N15
East Fm. of Gilmerton EH17	43	Q11
East Fettes Av. EH4	11	K18
East Fountainbridge EH3	6	L16
East Hannahfield, Bal. EH14	44	B9
East Hermitage Pl. EH6	12	O18
East Lillypot EH5	11	L19
East London St. EH7	20	M17
East Mkt. St. EH8	7	N16
East Mayfield EH9	32	N14
East Montgomery Pl. EH7	20	N17
East Newington Pl. EH9	32	N15
East Norton Pl. EH7	21	N17
East Parkside EH16	20	N15
East Preston St. EH8	20	N15
East Preston St. La. EH8	20	N15
East Preston St.		
East Restalrig Ter. EH6	12	O18
East Savile Rd. EH16	32	N14
East Sciennes St. EH9	20	N15
East Scotland St. La. EH3	20	M17
East Silvermills La. EH3	19	L17
East Suffolk Rd. EH16	33	O14
East Telferton EH7	22	Q17
East Trinity Rd. EH5	11	L19
East Way, The EH8	22	Q16
Easter Belmont Rd. EH12	18	H16
Easter Currie Ct., Currie EH14	38	E10
Easter Currie Cres., Currie EH14	38	E11
Easter Currie Pl., Currie EH14	38	E11
Easter Currie Ter., Currie EH14	38	E10
Easter Drylaw Av. EH4	10	J18
Easter Drylaw Bk. EH4	10	J18
Easter Drylaw Dr. EH4	10	J18
Easter Drylaw Gdns. EH4	10	J18
Easter Drylaw Gro. EH4	10	J18
Easter Drylaw Ln. EH4	10	J18
Easter Drylaw Pl. EH4	10	J18
Easter Drylaw Vw. EH4	10	J18
Easter Drylaw Way EH4	10	J18
Easter Haugh EH13	40	K12
Easter Hermitage EH6	13	O18
Easter Pk. Dr. EH4	9	G18
Easter Rd. EH6	12	O18
Easter Rd. EH7	21	N17
Easter Steil EH10	31	K13
Easter Warriston EH7	11	M18
Eastfield EH15	24	T16
Eastfield Gdns. EH15	24	T16
Eastfield Pl. EH15	24	T16
Eastfield Rd., Newbr. EH28	14	B15
Easthouses Ct., Dalk. EH22	50	V8
Easthouses Ind. Est.	50	V8
(Easth.), Dalk. EH22		
Easthouses Pl.	50	V8
(Easth.), Dalk. EH22		
Easthouses Rd.	50	V9
(Easth.), Dalk. EH22		

Street	Page	Ref
Easthouses Way	50	V9
(Easth.), Dalk. EH22		
Eden La. EH10	31	L14
Eden Ter. EH10	31	L14
Newbattle Ter.		
Edenhall Bk., Muss. EH21	25	W15
Edenhall Cres., Muss. EH21	25	W15
Edenhall Rd., Muss. EH21	25	W15
Edgefield Ind. Est., Loanh. EH20	47	P9
Edgefield Pl., Loanh. EH20	47	P8
Edgefield Rd., Loanh. EH20	47	P9
Edina Pl. EH7	21	O17
Edina St. EH7	20	N17
Edinburgh Airport EH12	14	A16
Edinburgh Pk. EH12	27	D15
Edinburgh Rd., Dalk. EH22	50	T10
Edinburgh Rd., Muss. EH21	24	T16
Edmonstone Av.	51	R12
(Dand.), Dalk. EH22		
Edmonstone Dr.	51	R12
(Dand.), Dalk. EH22		
Edmonstone Rd.	51	R12
(Dand.), Dalk. EH22		
Edmonstone Ter.	51	R12
(Dand.), Dalk. EH22		
Eglinton Cres. EH12	19	K16
Eglinton St. EH12	19	K16
Egypt Ms. EH10	32	M14
Eildon St. EH3	11	M18
Eildon Ter. EH3	11	L18
Elbe St. EH6	12	O19
Elcho Ter. EH15	23	S16
Elder St. EH1	7	M17
Elder St. E. EH1	7	M17
Eldindean Pl., Bonny. EH19	49	R8
Eldindean Rd., Bonny. EH19	49	R8
Eldindean Ter., Bonny. EH19	49	R8
Electra Pl. EH15	22	R17
Elgin Pl. EH12	19	K16
Elgin St. N. EH7	20	N17
Elgin St. S. EH7	20	N17
Elgin Ter. EH7	20	N17
Elizafield EH6	12	N18
Ellangowan Ter. EH16	33	O13
Ellen's Glen Rd. EH17	43	P11
Ellersly Rd. EH12	18	J16
Elliot Gdns. EH14	40	J12
Elliot Pk. EH14	40	J12
Elliot Pl. EH14	40	J12
Elliot Rd. EH14	40	J12
Elliot St. EH7	20	N17
Elm Pl. EH6	12	O18
Elm Row EH7	7	N17
Elm Row, Lass. EH18	49	R9
Elmfield Ct., Dalk. EH22	50	U10
Elmfield Pk., Dalk. EH22	50	U10
Elmfield Rd., Dalk. EH22	50	U10
Elmwood Ter. EH6	13	O18
Eltringham Gdns. EH14	30	J14
Eltringham Gro. EH14	30	J14
Eltringham Ter. EH14	30	J14
Engine Rd., Loanh. EH20	47	P8
Erskine Pl.	6	L16
Shandwick Pl.		
Esdaile EH9	32	M14
Esk Glades, Dalk. EH22	50	U10
Esk Pl., Dalk. EH22	50	T10
Eskbank Ct., Dalk. EH22	50	T10
Eskbank Rd., Bonny. EH19	49	S8
Eskbank Rd., Dalk. EH22	50	T9
Eskbank Ter., Dalk. EH22	50	T9
Eskdaill Ct., Dalk. EH22	50	U10
South St.		
Eskdaill St., Dalk. EH22	50	U10
Eskdale Ct., Bonny. EH19	49	R8
Eskdale Dr., Bonny. EH19	48	R8
Eskdale Ms., Muss. EH21	25	V15
Eskdale Ter., Bonny. EH19	49	R8
Eskfield Gro., Dalk. EH22	49	S9
Eskmill Vills., Muss. EH21	24	U15
Eskside, Dalk. EH22	50	T10
Ironmills Rd.		
Eskside E., Muss. EH21	25	V15
Eskside W., Muss. EH21	24	U15
Eskview Av., Muss. EH21	24	U15
Eskview Cres., Muss. EH21	24	U15
Eskview Gro., Dalk. EH22	50	T10
Eskview Gro., Muss. EH21	24	U15
Eskview Rd., Muss. EH21	24	U15
Eskview Ter., Muss. EH21	24	U15
Eskview Vills., Dalk. EH22	50	T9
Esplanade EH4	8	F20
Esplanade Ter. EH15	23	S16
Essendean Pl. EH4	16	F17
Essendean Ter. EH4	16	F17
Essex Brae EH4	8	E18
Essex Pk. EH4	8	E18
Essex Rd. EH4	8	E18
Esslemont Rd. EH16	32	N13
Ethel Ter. EH10	31	L13
Eton Ter. EH4	6	L17
Ettrick Gro. EH10	31	L15
Ettrick Rd. EH10	31	K14
Ettrickdale Pl. EH3	19	L17
Eva Pl. EH9	32	N13
Evans Gdns., Bonny. EH19	49	S8
Ewerland EH4	8	E18
Eyre Cres. EH3	20	M17
Eyre Pl. EH3	20	M17
Eyre Ter. EH3	20	M17
Fair-a-Far EH4	8	E19
Fair-a-Far Cotts. EH4	8	E19
Fair-a-Far Shot EH4	8	E19
Fairford Gdns. EH16	33	O13
Fairhaven Vills., Dalk. EH22	50	T9
Fairmile Av. EH10	41	L11
Fairview Rd., Newbr. EH28	14	A16
Fairways	24	U14
(Monk.), Muss. EH21		
Fala Ct. EH16	43	O11
Falcon Av. EH10	31	L14
Falcon Ct. EH10	31	L14
Falcon Gdns. EH10	31	L14
Falcon Rd. EH10	31	L14
Falcon Rd. W. EH10	31	L14
Falkland Gdns. EH12	17	G17
Farrer Gro. EH7	22	Q17
Farrer Ter. EH7	22	Q17
Fauldburn EH12	16	E17
Fauldburn Pk. EH12	16	E17
Featherhall Av. EH12	16	F15
Featherhall Cres. N. EH12	16	F15
Featherhall Cres. S. EH12	16	F15
Featherhall Gro. EH12	16	F15
Featherhall Pl. EH12	16	F15
Featherhall Rd. EH12	16	F15
Featherhall Ter. EH12	16	F15
Ferguson Ct., Muss. EH21	24	V14
Ferguson Dr., Muss. EH21	24	U14
Ferguson Gdns., Muss. EH21	24	U14
Ferguson Dr.		
Ferguson Grn., Muss. EH21	24	U14
Ferguson Vw., Muss. EH21	24	U14
Ferniehill Av. EH17	43	Q11
Ferniehill Dr. EH17	43	Q11
Ferniehill Gdns. EH17	43	Q12
Ferniehill Gro. EH17	43	Q12
Ferniehill Pl. EH17	43	Q11
Ferniehill Rd. EH17	43	Q11
Ferniehill Sq. EH17	43	Q11
Ferniehill St. EH17	43	Q12
Ferniehill Ter. EH17	43	Q11
Ferniehill Way EH17	43	Q12
Fernielaw Av. EH13	39	H11
Fernieside Av. EH17	43	Q12
Fernieside Cres. EH17	43	Q12
Fernieside Dr. EH17	43	Q12
Fernieside Gdns. EH17	43	Q12
Fernieside Gro. EH17	43	Q12
Ferry Rd. EH4	10	H18
Ferry Rd. EH5	10	K18
Ferry Rd. EH6	12	M19
Ferry Rd. Av. EH4	10	J18
Ferry Rd. Dr. EH4	10	J19
Ferry Rd. Gdns. EH4	10	J18
Ferry Rd. Gro. EH4	10	J18
Ferry Rd. Pl. EH4	10	J18
Ferryfield EH5	11	K19
Festival Sq. EH3	6	L16
Fettes Av. EH4	19	K17
Fettes Ri. EH4	11	K18
Fettes Row EH3	20	M17
Fidra Ct. EH4	9	H19
Figgate Bk. EH15	23	R17
Figgate La. EH15	22	R17
Figgate St. EH15	22	R17
Fillyside Av. EH7	22	Q17
Fillyside Rd. EH7	13	Q18
Fillyside Ter. EH7	13	Q18
Findhorn Pl. EH9	32	N14
Findlay Av. EH7	13	P18
Findlay Cotts. EH7	13	P18
Findlay Gdns. EH7	13	P18
Findlay Gro. EH7	13	P18
Findlay Medway EH7	13	P18
Fingal Pl. EH9	20	M15
Fingzies Pl. EH6	12	O18
Finlaggan Ct. EH12	16	E16
Craigievar Wynd		
Firrhill Cres. EH13	40	K12
Firrhill Dr. EH13	40	K12
Firrhill Ln. EH13	40	K12
First Gait	37	D12
(Ricc.), Currie EH14		
Fishers Wynd, Muss. EH21	24	U15
Fishmarket Sq. EH6	11	M20
Fishwives Causeway EH15	22	Q17
Fleshmarket Clo. EH1	7	M16
High St.		
Forbes Rd. EH10	31	L15
Forbes St. EH8	7	N15
Fords Rd. EH11	30	H14
Forres St. EH3	6	L17
Forrest Hill EH1	7	M16
Forrest Rd. EH1	7	M16
Forrester Pk. Av. EH12	28	F14
Forrester Pk. Dr. EH12	28	F14
Forrester Pk. Gdns. EH12	28	F14
Forrester Pk. Grn. EH12	29	G14
Forrester Pk. Gro. EH12	29	F14
Forrester Pk. Ln. EH12	29	F14
Forrester Rd. EH12	16	F16
Forteviot Ho. EH17	43	P12
Forth St. EH1	7	M17
Forth Vw. Av., Currie EH14	37	D10
Forth Vw. Cres.	51	R12
(Dand.), Dalk. EH22		
Forth Vw. Rd., Currie EH14	37	D10
Forthview Cres., Currie EH14	37	D10
Forthview Rd. EH4	18	J17
Forthview Ter. EH4	18	H17
Foulis Cres., Jun.Grn. EH14	39	F11
Foundry La., Loanh. EH20	48	P9
Fountain Pl., Loanh. EH20	47	P8
Fountainbridge EH3	6	L15
Fountainhall Rd. EH9	32	N14
Fourth Gait	37	D12
(Ricc.), Currie EH14		
Fowler Cres., Loanh. EH20	48	P8
Fowler Sq., Loanh. EH20	48	P8
Fowler Ter. EH11	31	K15
Fox Covert Av. EH12	17	G17
Fox Covert Gro. EH12	17	G17
Fox Spring Cres. EH10	40	K12
Fox Spring Ri. EH10	41	L12
Fraser Av. EH5	11	L19
Fraser Cres. EH5	11	L19
Fraser Gdns. EH5	11	L19
Fraser Gro. EH5	11	L19
Fraser Homes EH13	39	H12
Spylaw Bk. Rd.		
Frederick St. EH2	6	M17
Freelands Rd.	26	B14
(Ratho), Newbr. EH28		
Frogston Av. EH10	41	L11
Frogston Gdns. EH10	41	L11
Frogston Gro. EH10	41	M11
Frogston Rd. E. EH17	42	N10
Frogston Rd. W. EH10	41	L11
Frogston Ter. EH10	41	M11
Gabriel's Rd. EH2	7	M17
West Register St.		
Gabriel's Rd. EH3	19	L17
Galachlaw Shot EH10	41	M11
Galachlawside EH10	41	M11
Gallolee, The EH13	40	J11
Galt Av., Muss. EH21	25	X15
Galt Cres., Muss. EH21	25	X15
Gamekeeper's Ln. EH4	8	E19
Gamekeeper's Pk. EH4	8	E19
Gamekeeper's Rd. EH4	8	E19
Garden Ter. EH4	9	F18
Gardiner Gro. EH4	18	H17
Gardiner Rd. EH4	18	H17
Gardiner Ter. EH4	18	H17
Gardner St. EH7	21	O17
Lower London Rd.		
Gardner's Cres. EH3	6	L16
Garscube Ter. EH12	18	J16
Garvald Ct. EH16	42	O11

Street	Map	Grid
Gayfield Clo. EH1	20	N17
Gayfield Sq.		
Gayfield Pl. EH7	20	N17
Gayfield Pl. La. EH1	20	N17
Gayfield Sq. EH1	20	N17
Gayfield St. EH1	20	N17
Gaynor Av., Loanh. EH20	47	O8
General's Entry EH8	7	M16
Bristo Sq.		
George Av., Loanh. EH20	47	O8
George Cres., Loanh. EH20	47	P8
George Dr., Loanh. EH20	47	O8
George IV Bri. EH1	7	M16
George Sq. EH8	7	M15
George Sq. La. EH8	7	M15
George St. EH2	6	L16
George Ter., Loanh. EH20	47	O8
Gibb's Entry EH8	7	N16
Simon Sq.		
Gibraltar Ct., Dalk. EH22	50	U10
Gibraltar Gdns., Dalk. EH22	50	U10
Gibraltar Rd., Dalk. EH22	50	U10
Gibraltar Ter., Dalk. EH22	50	U10
Gibson Dr., Dalk. EH22	50	V10
Gibson St. EH7	12	N18
Gibson Ter. EH11	19	L15
Gifford Pk. EH8	7	N15
Gilberstoun EH15	23	S15
Gilberstoun Brig EH15	35	S15
Gilberstoun Ln. EH15	35	S15
Gilberstoun Pl. EH15	23	S15
Gilberstoun Wynd EH15	35	S15
Gilchrist's Entry EH1	20	M17
Leith St.		
Gilchrist's La. EH1	7	N17
Greenside Row		
Giles St. EH6	12	N19
Gillespie Cres. EH10	19	L15
Gillespie Pl. EH10	19	L15
Gillespie Rd. EH13	39	G11
Gillespie St. EH3	19	L15
Gillsland Pk. EH10	31	K14
Gillsland Rd. EH10	31	K14
Gilmerton Dykes Av. EH17	43	P11
Gilmerton Dykes Cres. EH17	43	P11
Gilmerton Dykes Dr. EH17	43	P11
Gilmerton Dykes Gdns. EH17	43	P11
Gilmerton Dykes Gro. EH17	43	P11
Gilmerton Dykes Ln. EH17	43	P11
Gilmerton Dykes Pl. EH17	43	P10
Gilmerton Dykes Rd. EH17	43	P11
Gilmerton Dykes St. EH17	43	P11
Gilmerton Dykes Ter. EH17	43	P11
Gilmerton Dykes Vw. EH17	43	P11
Gilmerton Pl. EH17	43	P11
Gilmerton Rd. EH16	33	O13
Gilmerton Rd. EH17	43	P12
Gilmerton Rd., Dalk. EH22	49	S10
Gilmerton Rd., Lass. EH18	51	Q11
Gilmerton Sta. Rd. EH17	43	Q10
Gilmore Pk. EH3	6	L15
Gilmore Pl. EH3	6	L15
Gilmore Pl. La. EH3	6	L15
Gilmour Rd. EH16	32	N14
Gilmour St. EH8	7	N16
Gilmour's Entry EH8	7	N16
Gilmour St.		
Gladstone Pl. EH6	13	O18
Gladstone Ter. EH9	20	N15
Glanville Pl. EH3	6	L17
Kerr St.		
Glasgow Rd. EH12	16	E15
Glasgow Rd., Newbr. EH28	14	A15
Glebe, The EH4	8	E19
Glebe Gdns. EH12	17	F15
Glebe Gro. EH12	17	F15
Glebe Pl. EH1	7	M16
High St.		
Glebe Pl., Lass. EH18	48	Q9
Glebe Rd. EH12	17	F15
Glebe St., Dalk. EH22	50	U10
Glebe Ter. EH12	17	F15
Glen St. EH3	6	M15
Glenallan Dr. EH16	33	O13
Glenallan Ln. EH16	33	O13
Glenalmond Ct. EH11	29	F13
Glenbrook, Bal. EH14	44	A8
Glenbrook Rd., Bal. EH14	44	A8
Glencairn Cres. EH12	19	K16
Glendevon Av. EH12	18	H15
Glendevon Gdns. EH12	18	H15
Glendevon Gro. EH12	18	H15
Glendevon Pk. EH12	18	H15
Glendevon Pl. EH12	18	H15
Glendevon Rd. EH12	18	H15
Glendevon Ter. EH12	18	H15
Glendinning Cres. EH16	42	O12
Glenesk Cres., Dalk. EH22	50	T9
Glenfinlas St. EH3	6	L16
Glengyle Ter. EH3	19	L15
Glenisla Gdns. EH9	32	M14
Glenisla Gdns. La. EH9	32	M14
Glenisla Gdns.		
Glenlea Cotts. EH11	30	J14
Glenlee Av. EH8	21	P16
Glenlee Gdns. EH8	21	P16
Glenlockhart Bk. EH14	30	J13
Glenlockhart Rd. EH10	30	J13
Glenlockhart Rd. EH14	30	J13
Glenlockhart Valley EH14	30	J13
Glenogle Pl. EH3	19	L17
Glenogle Rd. EH3	19	L17
Glenogle Ter. EH3	11	L18
Glenorchy Pl. EH1	7	N17
Greenside Row		
Glenorchy Ter. EH9	32	N14
Glenpark, Bal. EH14	44	A9
Glenure Ln. EH4	16	F17
Glenvarloch Cres. EH16	42	O12
Gloucester La. EH3	6	L17
Gloucester Pl. EH3	6	L17
Gloucester Sq. EH3	6	L17
Gloucester La.		
Gloucester St. EH3	6	L17
Goff Av. EH7	22	Q17
Gogar Mains Fm. Rd. EH12	15	C16
Gogar Sta. Rd. EH12	27	C15
Gogarbank EH12	27	D14
Gogarloch Haugh EH12	28	E15
Gogarloch Muir EH12	28	E15
Gogarloch Rd. EH12	28	E15
Gogarloch Syke EH12	28	E15
Gogarside Roundabout EH12	15	D15
Gogarstone Rd., Newbr. EH28	26	B15
Goldenacre Ter. EH3	11	L18
Goldie Ter., Loanh. EH20	47	O8
Golf Course Rd., Bonny. EH19	49	R8
Goose Grn. Av., Muss. EH21	25	V16
Goose Grn. Bri., Muss. EH21	25	V16
Goose Grn. Cres., Muss. EH21	25	V16
Goose Grn. Pl., Muss. EH21	25	V16
Goose Grn. Rd., Muss. EH21	25	V16
Gordon Ln. EH12	17	G16
Gordon Rd. EH12	17	G16
Gordon St. EH6	12	O18
Gordon Ter. EH16	33	O13
Gorgie Cotts. EH11	30	J14
Gorgie Pk. Clo. EH14	30	J14
Gorgie Pk. Rd. EH14	30	J14
Gorgie Rd. EH11	30	J15
Gosford Pl. EH6	12	M19
Gowanhill Rd., Currie EH14	36	B11
Gracefield Ct., Muss. EH21	24	U15
Fishers Wynd		
Gracemount Av. EH16	42	O12
Gracemount Dr. EH16	42	O11
Gracemount Pl. EH16	42	O11
Gracemount Rd. EH16	42	O11
Gracemount Sq. EH16	42	O11
Graham St. EH6	12	N19
Granby Rd. EH16	32	N14
Grandfield EH6	11	M19
Grandville EH6	11	M19
Grange Ct. EH9	32	N15
Causewayside		
Grange Cres. EH9	32	M14
Grange Ln. EH9	32	M14
Grange Ln. Gdns. EH9	32	M14·
Grange Rd. EH9	32	M15
Grange Ter. EH9	32	M14
Grant Av. EH13	39	H11
Granton Cres. EH5	10	K19
Granton Gdns. EH5	11	K19
Granton Gro. EH5	11	K19
Granton Mains Av. EH4	10	J19
Granton Mains Bk. EH4	10	J19
Granton Mains Brae EH4	10	J19
Granton Mains Ct. EH4	10	J19
Granton Mains E. EH4	10	J19
Granton Mains Gait EH4	10	J19
Granton Mains Vale EH4	10	J19
Granton Mains Wynd EH4	10	J19
Granton Medway EH5	10	K19
Granton Pk. Av. EH5	10	K20
Granton Pl. EH5	11	K19
Granton Rd. EH5	11	L19
Granton Sq. EH5	11	K20
Granton Ter. EH5	11	K19
Granton Vw. EH5	11	K19
Grantully Pl. EH9	32	N14
Granville Ter. EH10	31	L15
Grassmarket EH1	6	M16
Grays Ct. EH8	7	N16
Gray's Ln. EH10	31	K14
Great Cannon Bk. EH15	22	R17
Great Carleton Pl. EH16	34	R14
Great Carleton Sq. EH16	34	R14
Great Junct. St. EH6	12	N19
Great King St. EH3	6	M17
Great Michael Clo. EH6	12	M20
Newhaven Pl.		
Great Michael Ri. EH6	12	M19
Great Michael Sq. EH4	9	G18
Main St.		
Great Stuart St. EH3	6	L16
Green, The EH4	9	G18
Green, The, Bal. EH14	45	C8
Green St. EH7	20	M17
Green Way EH14	29	G13
Greenbank Av. EH10	31	L13
Greenbank Cres. EH10	41	L12
Greenbank Dr. EH10	31	K13
Greenbank Gdns. EH10	41	K12
Greenbank Gro. EH10	40	K12
Greenbank La. EH10	31	K13
Greenbank Ln. EH10	41	K12
Greenbank Pk. EH10	40	K12
Greenbank Pl. EH10	31	L13
Greenbank Ri. EH10	41	K12
Greenbank Rd. EH10	31	K13
Greenbank Row EH10	40	K12
Greenbank Ter. EH10	31	L13
Greendykes Av. EH16	34	Q14
Greendykes Dr. EH16	34	Q14
Greendykes Gdns. EH16	34	Q14
Greendykes Ho. EH16	34	Q14
Greendykes Ln. EH16	34	Q14
Greendykes Rd. EH16	34	Q14
Greendykes Ter. EH16	34	Q14
Greenend Dr. EH17	43	P12
Greenend Gdns. EH17	43	P12
Greenend Gro. EH17	43	P12
Greenfield Cres., Bal. EH14	45	C8
Greenfield Pk. (Monk.), Muss. EH21	24	U14
Greenfield Rd., Bal. EH14	45	C8
Greenhill Ct. EH10	31	L15
Greenhill Gdns. EH10	31	L15
Greenhill Pk. EH10	31	L14
Greenhill Pl. EH10	31	L14
Greenhill Ter. EH10	31	L15
Greenlaw Hedge EH13	40	K12
Greenlaw Rig EH13	40	K12
Greenmantle Ln. EH16	33	O13
Greenside Ct. EH1	7	N17
Greenside Row		
Greenside La. EH1	7	N17
Greenside Pl. EH1	7	N17
Greenside Row EH1	7	N17
Greyfriars Pl. EH1	7	M16
Candlemaker Row		
Grierson Av. EH5	11	L19
Grierson Cres. EH5	11	L19
Grierson Gdns. EH5	11	L19
Grierson Rd. EH5	11	K19
Grierson Sq. EH5	11	L19
Grierson Vills. EH5	11	L19
Grigor Av. EH4	10	J18
Grigor Dr. EH4	10	J18
Grigor Gdns. EH4	10	J18
Grigor Ter. EH4	10	J18
Grindlay St. EH3	6	L16
Grindlay St. Ct. EH3	6	L16
Groathill Av. EH4	18	J17
Groathill Gdns. E. EH4	18	J17
Groathill Gdns. W. EH4	18	J17
Groathill Rd. N. EH4	10	J18
Groathill Rd. S. EH4	18	J17
Grosvenor Cres. EH12	19	K16
Grosvenor Gdns. EH12	19	K16
Grosvenor St. EH12	19	L16

Street	Page	Grid
Hyvot Ln. EH17	43	P11
Hyvot Pk. EH17	43	P11
Hyvot Ter. EH17	43	P11
Hyvot Vw. EH17	43	P11
Hyvot's Bk. Av. EH17	43	Q11
Imperial Dock EH6	12	O20
Inchview Ter. EH7	22	Q17
India Bldgs. EH1	7	M16
Victoria St.		
India Pl. EH3	6	L17
India St. EH3	6	L17
Industrial Rd. EH6	12	O18
Industry Home EH6	12	N19
Industry La.		
Industry La. EH6	12	N19
Infirmary St. EH1	7	N16
Inglewood Pl. EH16	42	O12
Inglis Ct. EH1	6	M16
West Port		
Inglis Grn. Rd. EH14	30	H13
Ingliston, Newbr. EH28	14	A16
Ingliston Rd. (Inglis.), Newbr. EH28	14	A15
Inveralmond Dr. EH4	8	E19
Inveralmond Gdns. EH4	8	E19
Inveralmond Gro. EH4	8	E19
Inveravon Rd., Loanh. EH20	47	O9
Inveravon Ter., Muss. EH21	24	V15
Inveresk Brae, Muss. EH21	25	V15
Inveresk Gdns., Muss. EH21	24	T14
Inveresk Ind. Est., Muss. EH21	24	V15
Inveresk Mills Ind. Pk., Muss. EH21	24	U15
Inveresk Rd., Muss. EH21	25	V15
Inveresk Village Rd., Muss. EH21	25	V15
Inverleith Av. EH3	11	L18
Inverleith Av. S. EH3	11	L18
Inverleith Gdns. EH3	11	L18
Inverleith Gro. EH3	11	K18
Inverleith Pl. EH3	11	K18
Inverleith Pl. La. EH3	11	L18
Inverleith Row EH3	11	L18
Inverleith Ter. EH3	11	L18
Inverleith Ter. La. EH3	11	L18
Iona St. EH6	12	N18
Ironmills Rd., Dalk. EH22	50	T10
Ivanhoe Cres. EH16	33	O13
Ivy Ter. EH11	30	K15
Jamaica Ms. EH3	6	L17
Jamaica St. EH3	6	L17
Jamaica St. N. La. EH3	6	L17
Jamaica St. S. La. EH3	6	L17
James' Ct. EH1	7	M16
Lawnmarket		
James Craig Wk. EH1	7	M17
James Lean Av., Dalk. EH22	50	U10
James Leary Way, Bonny. EH19	49	S8
James St. EH15	23	S16
James St., Muss. EH21	25	V15
James St. La. EH15	23	S16
Jameson Pl. EH6	12	N18
Jane St. EH6	12	N18
Jane Ter. EH7	21	O17
Comely Grn. Cres.		
Janefield EH17	42	O10
Jarnac Ct., Dalk. EH22	50	U10
Jawbone Wk. EH3	7	M15
Jean Armour Av. EH16	33	O13
Jean Armour Dr., Dalk. EH22	50	V9
Jeffrey Av. EH4	18	H17
Jeffrey St. EH1	7	N16
Jessfield Ter. EH6	12	M19
Jewel, The EH15	34	R15
Jock's Lo. EH8	21	P17
John St. EH15	23	S16
John St. La. EH15	23	S16
John St. La. E. EH15	23	S16
John St. La.		
John St. La. W. EH15	23	S16
John's La. EH6	12	O19
John's Pl. EH6	12	O19
Johnsburn Grn., Bal. EH14	44	B9
Johnsburn Haugh, Bal. EH14	44	B9
Johnsburn Pk., Bal. EH14	44	B9
Johnsburn Rd., Bal. EH14	44	B9
Johnston Ter. EH1	6	M16
Joppa Gdns. EH15	23	S16
Joppa Gro. EH15	23	S16
Joppa Pans EH15	23	T16
Joppa Pk. EH15	23	S16
Joppa Rd. EH15	23	S16
Joppa Ter. EH15	23	S16
Jordan La. EH10	31	L14
Jubilee Rd. EH12	14	A16
Junction Pl. EH6	12	N18
Juniper Av., Jun.Grn. EH14	38	F11
Juniper Gdns., Jun.Grn. EH14	38	F11
Juniper Gro., Jun.Grn. EH14	38	F11
Juniper La., Jun.Grn. EH14	38	F11
Juniper Pk. Rd., Jun.Grn. EH14	38	F11
Juniper Pl., Jun.Grn. EH14	38	F11
Juniper Ter., Jun.Grn. EH14	38	F11
Juniperlee, Jun.Grn. EH14	38	F11
Kaimes Rd. EH12	17	G16
Kaimes Vw. (Dand.), Dalk. EH22	51	R12
Katesmill Rd. EH14	40	H12
Kedslie Pl. EH16	42	N12
Kedslie Rd. EH16	42	N12
Keir St. EH3	6	M16
Keith Cres. EH4	18	H17
Keith Row EH4	18	J17
Keith Ter. EH4	18	J17
Kekewich Av. EH7	22	Q17
Kemp Pl. EH3	19	L17
Kenilworth Dr. EH16	42	O12
Kenmure Av. EH8	21	P16
Kennington Av., Loanh. EH20	47	O8
Kennington Ter., Loanh. EH20	47	O8
Kerr Av., Dalk. EH22	50	T9
Kerr St. EH3	6	L17
Kerr's Wynd, Muss. EH21	25	V15
Kevock Rd., Lass. EH18	48	Q8
Kevock Vale Caravan Pk., Lass. EH18	48	R8
Kew Ter. EH12	18	K16
Kilchurn Ct. EH12	16	E16
Craigievar Wynd		
Kilgraston Ct. EH9	32	M14
Kilgraston Rd. EH9	32	M14
Kilmaurs Rd. EH16	33	O14
Kilmaurs Ter. EH16	33	O14
Kilncroftside EH14	30	H13
Kilwinning Pl., Muss. EH21	25	V15
Kilwinning St., Muss. EH21	25	V15
Kilwinning Ter., Muss. EH21	25	V15
Kincaid's Ct. EH1	20	M16
Kinellan Gdns. EH12	18	J16
Kinellan Rd. EH12	18	J16
King George V Pk., Bonny. EH19	49	R8
King Malcolm Clo. EH10	41	M11
King St. EH6	12	N19
King St., Muss. EH21	25	V15
Kinghorn Pl. EH6	12	M19
King's Bri. EH3	6	M16
King's Cramond EH4	8	E18
King's Haugh EH16	33	P14
King's Pl. EH15	22	R17
King's Rd. EH15	22	R17
King's Stables La. EH1	6	M16
King's Stables Rd. EH1	6	L16
King's Ter. EH15	22	Q17
Kingsburgh Rd. EH12	18	J16
Kingsknowe Av. EH14	29	H13
Kingsknowe Ct. EH14	29	G13
Kingsknowe Cres. EH14	29	H13
Kingsknowe Dr. EH14	29	H13
Kingsknowe Gdns. EH14	39	H12
Kingsknowe Gro. EH14	39	H12
Kingsknowe Pk. EH14	39	H12
Kingsknowe Pl. EH14	29	G13
Kingsknowe Rd. N. EH14	29	H13
Kingsknowe Rd. S. EH14	29	H13
Kingsknowe Ter. EH14	29	H13
Kingston Av. EH16	33	P13
Kinleith Ind. Est. EH14	38	E10
Kinnaird Pk. EH15	35	S14
Kinnear Rd. EH3	11	K18
Kippielaw Dr. (Easth.), Dalk. EH22	50	V9
Kippielaw Gdns. (Easth.), Dalk. EH22	50	V9
Kippielaw Medway (Easth.), Dalk. EH22	50	V9
Kippielaw Rd. (Easth.), Dalk. EH22	50	V9
Kippielaw Wk. (Easth.), Dalk. EH22	50	V9
Kirk Brae EH16	33	O13
Kirk Cramond EH4	8	E19
Kirk Ln. EH12	17	G15
Kirk Pk. EH16	42	O12
Kirk St. EH6	12	N18
Kirkgate EH6	20	N17
Leith Wk.		
Kirkgate EH12	42	O12
Kirkhill Dr. EH16	33	O14
Kirkhill Gdns. EH16	33	O15
Kirkhill Rd. EH16	33	O15
Kirkhill Ter. EH16	33	O15
Kirklands EH12	28	F15
Ladywell Av.		
Kirkwood Pl. EH7	21	O17
Lower London Rd.		
Kisimul Ct. EH12	16	E16
Craigievar Wynd		
Kittle Yards EH9	32	N14
Klondyke St. (Newcr.), Muss. EH21	35	T14
Klondyke Way (Newcr.), Muss. EH21	35	S14
Komarom Pl., Dalk. EH22	50	V10
Kyle Pl. EH7	20	N17
Montrose Ter.		
Lade, The, Bal. EH14	45	C8
Ladehead EH6	12	M18
Ladiemeadow EH12	29	G15
Lady Lawson St. EH3	6	M16
Lady Menzies Pl. EH7	21	O17
Lady Nairne Cres. EH8	22	P16
Lady Nairne Gro. EH8	22	P16
Lady Nairne Ln. EH8	22	P16
Lady Nairne Pl. EH8	22	P16
Lady Rd. EH16	33	O14
Lady Stair's Clo. EH1	7	M16
North Bk. St.		
Lady Wynd EH1	6	M16
Ladycroft, Bal. EH14	45	C9
Ladysmith Rd. EH9	32	N13
Ladywell, Muss. EH21	25	V15
Ladywell Av. EH12	28	F15
Ladywell Gdns. EH12	16	F15
Ladywell Ho. EH12	16	F15
Ladywell Rd. EH12	16	F15
Ladywell Way, Muss. EH21	24	U15
North High St.		
Laichfield EH14	30	H14
Laichpark Ln. EH14	30	H14
Chesser Ln.		
Laichpark Pl. EH14	30	H14
Laichpark Rd. EH14	30	H14
Laing Ter. EH15	23	S16
Lamb's Clo. EH8	7	N15
East Crosscauseway		
Lammermoor Ter. EH16	33	P13
Lampacre Rd. EH12	29	G15
Lanark Rd. EH13	39	F11
Lanark Rd. EH14	30	H13
Lanark Rd., Jun.Grn. EH14	39	F11
Lanark Rd. W., Bal. EH14	44	A9
Lanark Rd. W., Currie EH14	38	E10
Lang Linn Path EH10	32	M13
Lang Ln., Loanh. EH20	47	O9
Langlaw Rd., Dalk. EH22	50	V8
Langton Rd. EH9	32	N14
Lansbury Ct., Dalk. EH22	50	U10
Wheatsheaf La.		
Lansdowne Cres. EH12	19	K16
Lapicide Pl. EH6	12	N19
Larbourfield EH11	28	F13
Larchfield, Bal. EH14	44	C9
Larchfield Neuk, Bal. EH14	44	C9
Largo Pl. EH6	12	N19
Larkfield Dr., Dalk. EH22	49	S9
Larkfield Rd., Dalk. EH22	49	S9
Lasswade Bk. EH17	43	P11
Lasswade Gro. EH17	43	P11
Lasswade Rd. EH16	42	O12
Lasswade Rd. EH17	43	P11
Lasswade Rd., Dalk. EH22	49	S9
Lasswade Rd., Lass. EH18	48	Q9
Lasswade Rd., Loanh. EH20	48	P8

Street	Page	Grid
Marchhall Cres. EH16	33	O15
Marchhall Pl. EH16	33	O15
Marchhall Rd. EH16	33	O15
Marchmont Cres. EH9	32	M15
Marchmont Rd. EH9	32	M15
Marchmont St. EH9	32	M15
Mardale Cres. EH10	31	L14
Marine Dr. EH4	9	F19
Marine Dr. EH5	9	G19
Marine Esp. EH6	13	P19
Marionville Av. EH7	21	O17
Marionville Cres. EH7	21	P17
Marionville Dr. EH7	21	P17
Marionville Gro. EH7	21	P17
Marionville Medway EH7	21	P17
Marionville Pk. EH7	21	O17
Marionville Rd. EH7	21	O17
Marischal Pl. EH4	18	J17
Queensferry Rd.		
Maritime La. EH6	12	O19
Maritime St. EH6	12	O19
Market St. EH1	7	M16
Market St., Muss. EH21	24	U15
Marlborough St. EH15	23	R16
Marmion Cres. EH16	33	O13
Marshall Pl. EH7	21	O17
Lower London Rd.		
Marshall St. EH8	7	M16
Marshall's Ct. EH1	7	N17
Martin Gro., Bonny. EH19	49	S8
Martin Pl., Dalk. EH22	49	T9
Martin's Ct. EH6	12	O19
Bernard St.		
Maryburn Rd.	50	V8
(Easth.), Dalk. EH22		
Maryfield EH7	21	N17
Maryfield EH15	22	R17
Maryfield Pl. EH7	21	O17
Maryfield Pl., Bonny. EH19	49	S8
Mary's Pl. EH4	19	L17
Raeburn Pl.		
Marytree Ho. EH17	43	P12
Maulsford Av.	51	R12
(Dand.), Dalk. EH22		
Maurice Pl. EH9	32	M13
Mavisbank, Loanh. EH20	48	P8
Maxton Ct., Dalk. EH22	50	U10
Maxwell St. EH10	31	L14
May Ct. EH4	9	H19
Maybank Vills. EH12	16	F15
Victor Pk. Ter.		
Mayburn Av., Loanh. EH20	47	O9
Mayburn Bk., Loanh. EH20	47	O8
Mayburn Ct., Loanh. EH20	47	O8
Mayburn Cres., Loanh. EH20	47	O9
Mayburn Dr., Loanh. EH20	47	O9
Mayburn Gro., Loanh. EH20	47	O8
Mayburn Hill, Loanh. EH20	47	O8
Mayburn Ln., Loanh. EH20	47	O9
Mayburn Ter., Loanh. EH20	47	O9
Mayburn Vale, Loanh. EH20	47	O8
Mayburn Wk., Loanh. EH20	47	O8
Maybury Dr. EH12	16	E16
Maybury Gdns., Loanh. EH20	47	O9
Maybury Rd. EH4	16	E17
Maybury Rd. EH12	16	E16
Mayfield Av., Muss. EH21	24	U14
Mayfield Ct., Loanh. EH20	48	P8
High St.		
Mayfield Cres., Loanh. EH20	48	P8
Mayfield Cres., Muss. EH21	24	U14
Mayfield Gdns. EH9	32	N14
Mayfield Gdns. La. EH9	32	N14
Mayfield Pk., Muss. EH21	24	U14
Mayfield Pl. EH12	16	F15
Mayfield Pl., Muss. EH21	24	U14
Mayfield Rd. EH9	32	N14
Mayfield Ter. EH9	32	N14
Mayshade Rd., Loanh. EH20	47	O9
Mayville Gdns. EH5	11	M19
Mayville Gdns. E. EH5	11	M19
McDonald Pl. EH7	12	M18
McDonald Rd. EH7	12	M18
McDonald St. EH7	12	N18
McKelvie Par. EH5	11	L20
McLaren Rd. EH9	33	O14
McLaren Ter. EH11	19	L16
McLeod St. EH11	18	K15
McNeill Av., Loanh. EH20	47	O8
McNeill Pl., Loanh. EH20	47	O8
McNeill St. EH11	19	L15
McNeill Ter., Loanh. EH20	47	O8
McQuade St., Bonny. EH19	49	S8
Meadow La. EH8	7	M15
Meadow Pl. EH9	20	M15
Meadow Pl. La. EH9	20	M15
Meadow Pl. Rd. EH12	28	F15
Meadow Rd.	37	D12
(Ricc.), Currie EH14		
Meadowbank EH8	21	O17
Meadowbank Av. EH8	21	O17
Meadowbank Cres. EH8	21	O17
Meadowbank Pl. EH8	21	P17
London Rd.		
Meadowbank Ter. EH8	21	O17
Meadowfield Av. EH8	22	P16
Meadowfield Ct. EH8	22	P16
Meadowfield Dr. EH8	21	P16
Meadowfield Gdns. EH8	21	P15
Meadowfield Ter. EH8	21	P15
Meadowhouse Rd. EH12	17	G15
Meadowspot EH10	30	K13
Mearenside EH12	16	E16
Medwin Ho. EH11	28	F13
Meggetland Gate EH14	30	J14
Meggetland Ter. EH14	30	K14
Melbourne Pl. EH1	7	M16
George IV Bri.		
Melgund Ter. EH7	20	M17
Melville Cres. EH3	6	L16
Melville Dr. EH9	20	M15
Melville Dykes, Lass. EH18	49	R9
Melville Gate Rd., Dalk. EH22	49	S10
Melville Pl. EH3	6	L16
Queensferry St.		
Melville Rd., Dalk. EH22	50	T9
Melville St. EH3	6	L16
Melville St. La. EH3	6	L16
Melville Ter. EH9	20	M15
Melville Ter., Dalk. EH22	50	T9
Melville Vw., Lass. EH18	49	R8
Mentone Av. EH15	22	R17
Mentone Gdns. EH9	32	N14
Mentone Ter. EH9	32	N14
Merchant St. EH1	7	M16
Candlemaker Row		
Merchiston Av. EH10	31	L15
Merchiston Bk. Av. EH10	31	L14
Merchiston Bk. Gdns. EH10	31	L14
Merchiston Cres. EH10	31	L14
Merchiston Gdns. EH10	31	K14
Merchiston Gro. EH11	30	K15
Merchiston Ms. EH10	31	L15
Merchiston Pk. EH10	31	L15
Merchiston Pl. EH10	31	L15
Mertoun Pl. EH11	31	K15
Meuse La. EH2	7	M16
Mid Gillsland Rd. EH10	31	K14
Mid Gogarloch Syke EH12	28	E15
Mid Liberton EH16	33	O13
Mid New Cultins EH11	28	E13
Mid Steil EH10	31	K13
Middle Meadow Wk. EH3	7	M15
Middle Pier EH5	11	K20
South Gray St.		
Middleby Ct. EH9	32	N14
Middleby St. EH9	32	N14
Middlefield EH7	12	N18
Middleknowe EH14	38	F12
Middlepark EH14	38	F12
Westburn Middlefield		
Middleshot EH14	38	F12
Westburn Middlefield		
Midmar Av. EH10	32	M13
Midmar Dr. EH10	32	M13
Midmar Gdns. EH10	31	L13
Mill La. EH6	12	N19
Millar Cres. EH10	31	L14
Millar Pl. EH10	31	L14
Millar Pl. La. EH10	31	L14
Miller Row EH4	6	L16
Millerfield Pl. EH9	20	M15
Millerhill Rd., Dalk. EH22	35	R13
Millhill, Muss. EH21	25	V15
Millhill La., Muss. EH21	25	V15
Milnacre EH6	12	M19
Milton Cres. EH15	22	R15
Milton Dr. EH15	23	S16
Milton Gdns. N. EH15	22	R15
Milton Gdns. S. EH15	22	R15
Milton Gro. EH15	24	T16
Milton Link EH15	23	S15
Milton Rd. EH15	22	R15
Milton Rd. E. EH15	23	S15
Milton Rd. W. EH15	22	Q15
Milton St. EH8	21	O17
Milton Ter. EH15	24	T16
Minto St. EH9	32	N15
Mitchell St. EH6	12	O19
Mitchell St., Dalk. EH22	50	T10
Moat Dr. EH14	30	J14
Moat Pl. EH14	30	J14
Moat St. EH14	30	J14
Moat Ter. EH14	30	J14
Moira Pk. EH7	22	Q17
Moira Ter. EH7	22	Q17
Moncreiffe Ho. EH17	43	P12
Moncrieff Ter. EH9	32	N15
Monkbarns Gdns. EH16	42	O12
Monktonhall Pl., Muss. EH21	24	U14
Monktonhall Ter., Muss. EH21	24	U14
Monkwood Ct. EH9	32	M14
Monmouth Ter. EH3	11	L18
Montagu Ter. EH3	11	L18
Montague St. EH8	7	N15
Montgomery St. EH7	20	N17
Montgomery St. La. EH7	20	N17
Montpelier EH10	31	L15
Montpelier Pk. EH10	31	L15
Montpelier Ter. EH10	31	L15
Montrose Ter. EH7	20	N17
Moorfield Cotts., Dalk. EH22	51	S12
Moray Pl. EH3	6	L17
Moredun Dykes Rd. EH17	43	P11
Moredun Ho. EH17	43	P12
Moredun Pk. Ct. EH17	43	P12
Moredun Pk. Dr. EH17	43	P12
Moredun Pk. Gdns. EH17	43	P12
Moredun Pk. Grn. EH17	43	Q12
Moredun Pk. Gro. EH17	43	Q11
Moredun Pk. Ln. EH17	43	P12
Moredun Pk. Rd. EH17	43	P12
Moredun Pk. St. EH17	43	P12
Moredun Pk. Vw. EH17	43	Q12
Moredun Pk. Wk. EH17	43	Q12
Moredun Pk. Way EH17	43	P12
Moredunvale Bk. EH17	43	P12
Moredunvale Grn. EH17	43	P12
Moredunvale Gro. EH17	43	P12
Moredunvale Ln. EH17	43	P12
Moredunvale Pk. EH17	43	P12
Moredunvale Pl. EH17	43	P12
Moredunvale Rd. EH17	43	P12
Moredunvale Vw. EH17	43	P12
Moredunvale Way EH17	43	P12
Morningside Ct. EH10	31	L13
Morningside Gdns. EH10	31	K13
Morningside Gro. EH10	31	K13
Morningside Pk. EH10	31	L14
Morningside Pl. EH10	31	L14
Morningside Rd. EH10	31	L14
Morningside Ter. EH10	31	L14
Morrison Circ. EH3	19	L16
Morrison Cres.		
Morrison Cres. EH3	6	L15
Morrison St. EH3	6	L16
Morton St. EH15	23	S16
Mortonhall Gate EH16	42	N11
Mortonhall Pk. Av. EH17	42	N11
Mortonhall Pk. Bk. EH17	42	O11
Mortonhall Pk. Cres. EH17	42	O11
Mortonhall Pk. Dr. EH17	42	O11
Mortonhall Pk. Gdns. EH17	42	N11
Mortonhall Pk. Grn. EH17	42	N11
Mortonhall Pk. Gro. EH17	42	N11
Mortonhall Pk. Ln. EH17	42	N11
Mortonhall Pk. Pl. EH17	42	O11
Mortonhall Pk. Ter. EH17	42	O11
Mortonhall Pk. Vw. EH17	42	N11
Mortonhall Pk. Way EH17	42	N11
Mortonhall Rd. EH9	32	M14
Morven St. EH4	16	F17
Mossgiel Wk. EH16	33	O13
Moston Ter. EH9	32	N14
Mound, The EH1	6	M16
Mound, The EH2	6	M16
Mound Pl. EH1	6	M16
Mount Gra. EH9	32	M14
Mount Lo. Pl. EH15	23	R16
Mount Vernon Rd. EH16	42	O12
Mountcastle Bk. EH8	22	Q16

Mountcastle Cres. EH8	22	Q16
Mountcastle Dr. N. EH8	22	Q16
Mountcastle Dr. N. EH15	22	Q16
Mountcastle Dr. S. EH15	22	Q16
Mountcastle Gdns. EH8	22	Q16
Mountcastle Grn. EH8	22	Q16
Mountcastle Gro. EH8	22	Q16
Mountcastle Ln. EH8	22	Q16
Mountcastle Pk. EH8	22	Q16
Mountcastle Cres.		
Mountcastle Pl. EH8	22	Q17
Mountcastle Ter. EH8	22	Q16
Mounthooly Ln. EH10	41	M11
Mountjoy Ter., Muss. EH21	25	V16
Mucklets Av., Muss. EH21	24	U14
Mucklets Ct., Muss. EH21	24	U14
Mucklets Cres., Muss. EH21	24	U14
Mucklets Dr., Muss. EH21	24	U14
Mucklets Pl., Muss. EH21	24	U14
Muir Wd. Cres., Currie EH14	38	E11
Muir Wd. Dr., Currie EH14	38	E11
Muir Wd. Gro., Currie EH14	38	E11
Muir Wd. Pl., Currie EH14	38	E11
Muir Wd. Rd., Currie EH14	38	E11
Muirdale Ter. EH4	18	H17
Muirend Av., Jun.Grn. EH14	39	G12
Muirfield Gdns., Loanh. EH20	47	P8
Muirhouse Av. EH4	10	H18
Muirhouse Bk. EH4	9	H18
Muirhouse Cres. EH4	10	H19
Muirhouse Dr. EH4	9	H19
Muirhouse Gdns. EH4	9	H19
Muirhouse Grn. EH4	9	H18
Muirhouse Gro. EH4	9	H19
Muirhouse Ln. EH4	9	H19
Muirhouse Medway EH4	9	H18
Muirhouse Pk. EH4	9	H19
Muirhouse Parkway EH4	9	H19
Muirhouse Pl. E. EH4	10	H18
Muirhouse Pl. W. EH4	10	H18
Muirhouse Ter. EH4	9	H18
Muirhouse Vw. EH4	9	H19
Muirhouse Way EH4	10	H18
Muirpark, Dalk. EH22	50	T9
Muirside EH13	40	K11
Mulberry Pl. EH6	12	M19
Newhaven Rd.		
Munro Dr. EH13	39	H11
Munro Pl. EH3	11	M18
Canonmills		
Murano Pl. EH7	20	N17
Murdoch Ter. EH11	19	L15
Murieston Cres. EH11	19	K15
Murieston Cres. La. EH11	19	K15
Murieston La. EH11	19	K15
Murieston Pl. EH11	19	K15
Murieston Rd. EH11	19	K15
Murieston Ter. EH11	19	K15
Murray Cotts. EH12	16	F15
Murrayburn App. EH14	28	F13
Murrayburn Dr. EH14	28	F13
Murrayburn Gdns. EH14	29	G13
Murrayburn Gate EH14	28	F13
Murrayburn Grn. EH14	29	G13
Murrayburn Gro. EH14	29	G13
Murrayburn Pk. EH14	29	F13
Murrayburn Pl. EH14	29	F13
Murrayburn Rd. EH14	29	F13
Murrayfield Av. EH12	18	J16
Murrayfield Dr. EH12	18	J16
Murrayfield Gdns. EH12	18	J16
Murrayfield Pl. EH12	18	J16
Murrayfield Rd. EH12	18	J16
Murrays, The EH17	43	P10
Murrays Brae, The EH17	43	P10
Musselburgh Rd. EH15	23	S16
Musselburgh Rd., Dalk. EH22	50	U10
Myreside Ct. EH10	31	K13
Myreside Rd. EH10	31	K14
Myrtle Ter. EH11	30	K15
Nantwich Dr. EH7	13	Q18
Napier Rd. EH10	31	K14
Neidpath Ct. EH12	16	E16
Craigievar Wynd		
Nellfield EH16	43	O12
Nelson Pl. EH3	6	M17
Dublin Meuse		
Nelson St. EH3	6	M17
Nether Craigour EH17	34	P13

Nether Craigwell EH8	7	N16
Nether Currie Cres.,	38	E11
Currie EH14		
Nether Currie Pl.,	38	E11
Currie EH14		
Nether Currie Rd.,	38	E11
Currie EH14		
Nether Lennie EH12	15	C18
Netherbank EH16	42	N11
Netherbank Vw. EH16	42	N11
Netherby Rd. EH5	11	L19
New Arthur Pl. EH8	7	N16
New Belfield EH8	22	Q16
New Bells Ct. EH6	12	O19
New Broompark EH5	10	K20
New Broughton EH3	7	M17
New John's Pl. EH8	7	N15
New Lairdship Pl. EH11	29	F14
New Lairdship Yards EH11	29	F14
New La. EH6	12	M19
New Mart Rd. EH14	30	H14
New Meadowspott, Dalk. EH22	50	T9
Waverley Rd.		
New Morrison St. EH3	6	L16
New Orchardfield EH6	12	N18
New Skinners Clo. EH1	7	N16
Blackfriars St.		
New St. EH8	7	N16
New St. EH17	43	P11
New St., Muss. EH21	24	U15
New Swanston EH10	40	K11
New Twr. Pl. EH15	22	R17
Figgate La.		
Newbattle Abbey Cres.,	50	T8
Dalk. EH22		
Newbattle Rd., Dalk. EH22	50	T9
Newbattle Ter. EH10	31	L14
Newbigging, Muss. EH21	25	V15
Newcraighall Dr.	35	S14
(Newcr.), Muss. EH21		
Newcraighall Rd. EH15	35	R14
Newcraighall Rd., Muss. EH21	35	S14
Newhailes Av., Muss. EH21	24	U15
Newhailes Cres., Muss. EH21	24	T15
Newhailes Rd., Muss. EH21	24	T15
Newhaven Main St. EH6	11	M20
Newhaven Pl. EH6	12	M20
Newhaven Rd. EH6	12	M19
Newington Rd. EH9	32	N15
Newkirkgate EH6	12	N18
Newlands Pk. EH9	32	N14
Mayfield Gdns.		
Newmarket Rd. EH14	30	J14
Newmills Av., Bal. EH14	45	C10
Newmills Cres., Bal. EH14	45	C10
Newmills Gro., Bal. EH14	45	C10
Newmills Rd., Bal. EH14	45	C10
Newmills Rd., Dalk. EH22	50	U10
Newmills Ter., Dalk. EH22	50	U10
James Lean Av.		
Newtoft St. EH17	43	Q11
Newton Ch. Rd.	51	R12
(Dand.), Dalk. EH22		
Newton St. EH11	30	K15
Newton St.	50	V8
(Easth.), Dalk. EH22		
Newton Village, Dalk. EH22	51	S12
Nicolson Sq. EH8	7	N16
Nicolson St. EH8	7	N16
Niddrie Cotts. EH15	35	S14
Niddrie Fm. Gro. EH16	34	Q14
Niddrie Ho. Av. EH16	34	Q14
Niddrie Ho. Dr. EH16	34	R14
Niddrie Ho. Gdns. EH16	34	R14
Niddrie Ho. Gro. EH16	34	R14
Niddrie Ho. Pk. EH16	34	Q14
Niddrie Ho. Sq. EH16	34	R14
Niddrie Ho. Pk.		
Niddrie Mains Ct. EH16	34	R14
Niddrie Mains Dr. EH16	34	Q14
Niddrie Mains Rd. EH15	34	Q14
Niddrie Mains Rd. EH16	34	P14
Niddrie Mains Ter. EH16	34	Q14
Niddrie Marischal Cres. EH16	34	Q14
Niddrie Marischal Dr. EH16	34	Q14
Niddrie Marischal Gdns.		
EH16	34	Q14
Niddrie Marischal Grn. EH16	34	Q14
Niddrie Marischal Gro. EH16	34	R14
Niddrie Marischal Ln. EH16	34	Q14
Niddrie Marischal Pl. EH16	34	Q14

Niddrie Marischal Rd. EH16	34	R14
Niddrie Marischal St. EH16	34	Q14
Niddrie Mill Av. EH15	34	R14
Niddrie Mill Cres. EH15	34	R15
Niddrie Mill Dr. EH15	34	R14
Niddrie Mill Gro. EH15	34	R14
Niddrie Mill Pl. EH15	34	R14
Niddrie Mill Ter. EH15	34	R14
Niddry St. EH1	7	M16
Niddry St. S. EH1	7	M16
Cowgate		
Nigel Ln. EH16	42	O12
Nile Gro. EH10	31	L14
Nisbet Ct. EH7	13	O18
Niven's Knowe Rd., Loanh.	47	N8
EH20		
Nivenknowe Caravan Pk.,	47	N8
Loanh. EH20		
Noble Pl. EH6	13	O18
North Bk. St. EH1	20	M16
North Bri. EH1	7	M16
North Bri. Arc. EH1	7	M16
North Bri.		
North Bughtlin Bk. EH12	16	E17
North Bughtlin Brae EH12	16	E17
North Bughtlin Gate EH12	16	E17
North Bughtlin Neuk EH12	16	E17
North Bughtlin Pl. EH12	16	E17
North Bughtlin Rd. EH12	16	E17
North Bughtlinfield EH12	16	E17
North Bughtlinrig EH12	16	E17
North Bughtlinside EH12	16	E17
North Cairntow EH16	33	P15
North Castle St. EH2	6	L17
North Charlotte St. EH2	6	L16
North E. Circ. Pl. EH3	6	L17
North Fort St. EH6	12	N19
North Grns. EH15	34	R15
North Gyle Av. EH12	16	E15
North Gyle Dr. EH12	16	E16
North Gyle Fm. Ct. EH12	16	E15
North Gyle Fm. La. EH12	16	E15
North Gyle Gro. EH12	16	E16
North Gyle Ln. EH12	16	E16
North Gyle Pk. EH12	16	E16
North Gyle Rd. EH12	16	E16
North Gyle Ter. EH12	16	E15
North High St., Muss. EH21	24	U15
North Hillhousefield EH6	12	N19
North Junct. St. EH6	12	N19
North Leith Mill EH6	12	N19
North Leith Sands EH6	12	N19
North Meadow Wk. EH3	6	M15
North Meadow Wk. EH8	6	M15
North Meggetland EH14	30	K14
North Pk. Ter. EH4	19	L17
North Peffer Pl. EH16	33	P14
North Richmond St. EH8	20	N16
West Adam St.		
North St. Andrew La. EH2	7	M17
North St. Andrew St.		
North St. Andrew St. EH2	7	M17
North St. David St. EH2	6	M17
North Wk., The EH10	31	L13
North Way, The EH8	22	P16
North Werber Pk. EH4	10	K18
North Werber Pl. EH4	10	K18
North Werber Rd. EH4	10	K18
North W. Circ. Pl. EH3	6	L17
North Wynd, Dalk. EH22	50	U10
Northcote St. EH11	19	K15
Northfield Av. EH8	22	P16
Northfield Bdy. EH8	22	P17
Northfield Circ. EH8	22	P16
Northfield Cres. EH8	22	P16
Northfield Dr. EH8	22	Q16
Northfield Fm. Av. EH8	22	Q16
Northfield Fm. Rd. EH8	22	Q16
Northfield Gdns. EH8	22	Q16
Northfield Gro. EH8	22	Q16
Northfield Pk. EH8	22	Q16
Northfield Pk. Gro. EH8	22	Q16
Northfield Rd. EH8	22	P16
Northfield Sq. EH8	22	Q16
Northfield Ter. EH8	21	P16
Willowbrae Rd.		
Northlawn Ter. EH4	9	G18
Northumberland Pl. EH3	6	M17
Northumberland St.		
Northumberland Pl. La. EH3	6	M17
Northumberland St. EH3	6	M17

Name	Page	Grid
Northumberland St. N. E. La. EH3	6	M17
Northumberland St. N. W. La. EH3	6	M17
Northumberland St. S. E. La. EH3	6	M17
Northumberland St. S. W. La. EH3	6	M17
Northview Ct. EH4	10	H19
Norton Pk. EH7	21	O17
Oak La. EH12	17	G17
Oakfield Pl. EH8	7	N16
Oakville Ter. EH6	13	O18
Observatory Grn. EH9	32	N13
Observatory Rd. EH9	32	N13
Ochiltree Gdns. EH16	33	P13
Ogilvie Ter. EH11	31	K14
Old Assembly Clo. EH1	7	M16
High St.		
Old Broughton EH3	7	M17
Old Burdiehouse Rd. EH17	42	O10
Old Ch. La. EH15	21	P15
Old Dalkeith Rd. EH16	33	O14
Old Dalkeith Rd. EH17	33	O14
Old Dalkeith Rd. (Dand.), Dalk. EH22	51	R12
Old Edinburgh Rd., Dalk. EH22	50	T10
Old Fm. Av. EH13	40	H12
Old Fm. Pl. EH13	40	H12
Old Fishmarket Clo. EH1	7	M16
Old Kirk Rd. EH12	17	G16
Old Mill La. EH16	33	O13
Old Newmills Rd., Bal. EH14	45	C10
Old Quadrangle EH1	7	M16
South Bri.		
Old Tolbooth Wynd EH8	7	N16
Olive Bk. Rd., Muss. EH21	24	U15
Orchard Bk. EH4	18	K17
Orchard Brae EH4	19	K17
Orchard Brae Av. EH4	19	K17
Orchard Brae Gdns. EH4	19	K17
Orchard Brae Gdns. W. EH4	18	K17
Orchard Brae W. EH4	19	K17
Orchard Brae		
Orchard Cres. EH4	18	J17
Orchard Dr. EH4	18	J17
Orchard Gro. EH4	19	K17
Orchard Pl. EH4	19	K17
Orchard Rd. EH4	18	K17
Orchard Rd. S. EH4	18	J17
Orchard Ter. EH4	18	K17
Orchard Toll EH4	18	K17
Orchard Vw., Dalk. EH22	49	T9
Orchardfield Av. EH12	17	F15
Orchardfield La. EH6	12	N18
Orchardhead Ln. EH16	42	O12
Orchardhead Rd. EH16	42	O12
Ormelie Ter. EH15	23	S16
Ormidale Ter. EH12	18	J16
Ormiston Ter. EH12	17	F15
Orrok Pk. EH16	33	O13
Orwell Pl. EH11	19	K15
Orwell Ter. EH11	19	K15
Osborne Ter. EH12	19	K16
Oswald Ct. EH9	32	M14
Oswald Rd. EH9	32	M14
Oswald Ter. EH12	16	F15
Otterburn Pk. EH14	40	H12
Oxcraig St. EH5	11	K20
Oxford St. EH8	20	N15
Oxford Ter. EH4	6	L17
Oxgangs Av. EH13	40	K11
Oxgangs Bk. EH13	40	K11
Oxgangs Brae EH13	40	K11
Oxgangs Bdy. EH13	40	K11
Oxgangs Cres. EH13	40	K12
Oxgangs Dr. EH13	40	K12
Oxgangs Fm. Av. EH13	40	K11
Oxgangs Fm. Dr. EH13	40	K11
Oxgangs Fm. Gdns. EH13	40	K11
Oxgangs Fm. Gro. EH13	40	K11
Oxgangs Fm. Ln. EH13	40	K11
Oxgangs Fm. Ter. EH13	40	K11
Oxgangs Gdns. EH13	40	K12
Oxgangs Grn. EH13	40	K12
Oxgangs Gro. EH13	40	K12
Oxgangs Hill EH13	41	K12
Oxgangs Ln. EH13	40	K12
Oxgangs Medway EH13	40	K11
Oxgangs Pk. EH13	40	K11
Oxgangs Path EH13	40	K11
Oxgangs Brae		
Oxgangs Path E. EH13	40	K11
Oxgangs Pl. EH13	40	K12
Oxgangs Ri. EH13	40	K12
Oxgangs Rd. EH10	40	K11
Oxgangs Rd. EH13	40	K11
Oxgangs Rd. N. EH13	40	K11
Oxgangs Rd. N. EH14	40	J12
Oxgangs Row EH13	40	K11
Oxgangs St. EH13	40	K11
Oxgangs Ter. EH13	40	K11
Oxgangs Vw. EH13	40	K11
Paddock, The, Muss. EH21	25	V16
Balcarres Rd.		
Paddockholm, The EH12	17	G15
Paisley Av. EH8	21	P16
Paisley Cres. EH8	21	P16
Paisley Dr. EH8	21	P16
Paisley Gdns. EH8	21	P16
Paisley Gro. EH8	21	P16
Paisley Ter. EH8	21	P16
Palmer Pl., Currie EH14	37	D10
Palmer Rd., Currie EH14	37	D11
Palmerston Pl. EH12	19	K16
Palmerston Pl. La. EH12	19	L16
Palmerston Pl.		
Palmerston Rd. EH9	32	M15
Pankhurst Ln., Dalk. EH22	50	V10
Panmure Pl. EH3	6	M15
Pape's Cotts. EH12	18	J16
Paradykes Av., Loanh. EH20	47	O8
Park Av. EH15	22	R16
Park Av., Loanh. EH20	47	O8
Park Av., Muss. EH21	25	W15
Park Ct., Muss. EH21	25	W15
Park Cres. EH16	42	O12
Park Cres., Bonny. EH19	49	R8
Park Cres., Loanh. EH20	47	O8
Park Gdns. EH16	42	O12
Park Gdns., Muss. EH21	25	W15
Park Gro. EH16	42	O12
Park Gro. Pl., Muss. EH21	25	W15
Park Gro. Ter., Muss. EH21	25	W15
Park La., Dalk. EH22	50	T9
Park La., Muss. EH21	25	W15
Park Pl. EH6	11	M19
Park Rd. EH6	11	M19
Park Rd., Bonny. EH19	49	R8
Park Rd., Dalk. EH22	50	T9
Park Ter. (Newcr.), Muss. EH21	35	T14
Park Vw., Loanh. EH20	47	O8
Park Vw., Muss. EH21	25	W15
Park Vw. (Newcr.), Muss. EH21	35	S14
Parker Av. EH7	22	Q17
Parker Rd. EH7	22	Q17
Parker Ter. EH7	22	Q17
Parkgrove Av. EH4	16	F17
Parkgrove Bk. EH4	16	F17
Parkgrove Cres. EH4	16	F17
Parkgrove Dr. EH4	16	F17
Parkgrove Gdns. EH4	16	F17
Parkgrove Grn. EH4	16	F17
Parkgrove Ln. EH4	16	F17
Parkgrove Neuk EH4	16	F17
Parkgrove Path EH4	16	F17
Parkgrove Ter.		
Parkgrove Pl. EH4	16	F17
Parkgrove Rd. EH4	16	F17
Parkgrove Row EH4	16	F17
Parkgrove St. EH4	16	F17
Parkgrove Ter. EH4	16	F17
Parkgrove Vw. EH4	16	F17
Parkhead Av. EH11	29	G13
Parkhead Cres. EH11	29	G13
Parkhead Dr. EH11	29	G13
Parkhead Gdns. EH11	29	G13
Parkhead Gro. EH11	29	G13
Parkhead Ln. EH11	29	G13
Parkhead Pl. EH11	29	G13
Parkhead St. EH11	29	G13
Parkhead Ter. EH11	29	G13
Parkhead Vw. EH11	29	G13
Parkside Pl., Dalk. EH22	50	U10
Parkside St. EH8	7	N15
Parkside Ter. EH16	20	N15
Parkvale Pl. EH6	13	O18
Parliament Pl. EH6	12	N19
Parliament St.		
Parliament Sq. EH1	7	M16
Parliament Sq. EH6	12	M20
Newhaven Pl.		
Parliament St. EH6	12	N19
Parrotshot EH15	34	R15
Parsonage, Muss. EH21	25	V15
Parsons Grn. Ter. EH8	21	P17
Patie's Rd. EH14	40	J12
Patrick Geddes Steps EH1	20	M16
Patriothall EH3	19	L17
Hamilton Pl.		
Pattison St. EH6	12	O19
Peacock Ct. EH6	12	M20
Newhaven Pl.		
Peacocktail Clo. EH15	35	R14
Pearce Av. EH12	16	F16
Pearce Gro. EH12	16	F16
Pearce Rd. EH12	16	F16
Peatville Gdns. EH14	29	H13
Peatville Ter. EH14	29	H13
Peel Ter. EH9	32	N14
Peffer Bk. EH16	33	P14
Peffer Pl. EH16	33	P14
Peffer St. EH16	33	P14
Peffermill Ct. EH16	33	P14
Peffermill Rd. EH16	33	O14
Peggy's Mill Rd. EH4	8	E18
Pembroke Pl. EH12	19	K16
Pendreich Av., Bonny. EH19	49	S8
Pendreich Dr., Bonny. EH19	49	S8
Pendreich Gro., Bonny. EH19	49	S8
Pendreich Ter., Bonny. EH19	49	S8
Pendreich Vw., Bonny. EH19	49	S8
Pennywell Cotts. EH4	10	H19
Pennywell Ct. EH4	10	H19
Pennywell Gdns. EH4	9	H19
Pennywell Gro. EH4	10	H19
Pennywell Medway EH4	9	H19
Pennywell Pl. EH4	10	H19
Pennywell Rd. EH4	10	H19
Pennywell Vills. EH4	10	H19
Pentland Av. EH13	39	H11
Pentland Av., Currie EH14	37	D10
Pentland Cres. EH10	41	L12
Pentland Dr. EH10	41	K11
Pentland Gdns. EH10	41	L12
Pentland Gro. EH10	41	L12
Pentland Ind. Est., Loanh. EH20	47	N8
Pentland Rd. EH10	46	M9
Pentland Rd. EH13	39	H12
Pentland Rd., Bonny. EH19	48	R8
Pentland Rd., Loanh. EH20	46	M9
Pentland Ter. EH10	41	L12
Pentland Vw. EH10	41	L11
Pentland Vw., Currie EH14	37	D10
Pentland Vw., Dalk. EH22	50	V9
Pentland Vw. Ct., Currie EH14	37	D10
Pentland Vills., Jun.Grn. EH14	38	F11
Juniper Av.		
Perdrixknowe EH14	30	J14
Persevere Ct. EH6	12	N19
Perth St. EH3	19	L17
Pettigrew's Clo., Dalk. EH22	50	U10
Peveril Ter. EH16	42	O12
Picardy Pl. EH1	7	M17
Pier Pl. EH6	11	M20
Piersfield Gro. EH8	21	P17
Piersfield Pl. EH8	21	P17
Piersfield Ter. EH8	21	P17
Piershill La. EH8	21	P17
Piershill Pl. EH8	21	P17
Piershill Sq. E. EH8	21	P17
Piershill Sq. W. EH8	21	P17
Piershill Ter. EH8	21	P17
Pillars, The EH17	43	P12
Pilrig Cotts. EH6	12	N18
Pilrig Gdns. EH6	12	N18
Pilrig Glebe EH6	12	N18
Pilrig Ho. Clo. EH6	12	N18
Pilrig Pl. EH6	12	N18
Pilrig St. EH6	12	N18
Pilton Av. EH5	10	K19
Pilton Cres. EH5	10	K19
Pilton Dr. EH5	10	K19
Pilton Dr. N. EH5	10	K19
Pilton Gdns. EH5	10	K19

Street	Page	Grid
Pilton Ln. EH5	10	K19
Pilton Pk. EH5	10	K19
Pilton Pl. EH5	10	K19
Pinkhill EH12	17	G15
Pinkie Av., Muss. EH21	25	W15
Pinkie Dr., Muss. EH21	25	W15
Pinkie Hill Cres., Muss. EH21	25	W15
Pinkie Pl., Muss. EH21	25	W15
Pinkie Rd., Muss. EH21	25	V15
Pinkie Ter., Muss. EH21	25	W15
Pipe La. EH15	22	R17
Pipe St. EH15	22	R17
Pirniefield Bk. EH6	13	P18
Pirniefield Gdns. EH6	13	P18
Pirniefield Gro. EH6	13	P18
Pirniefield Pl. EH6	13	P18
Pirniefield Ter. EH6	13	P18
Pirrie St. EH6	12	N18
Pitlochry Pl. EH7	21	O17
Pitsligo Rd. EH10	31	L14
Pitt St. EH6	12	N19
Pittencrieff Ct. EH6	11	M19
Craighall Ter.		
Pittville St. EH15	23	R16
Pittville St. La. EH15	23	R16
Place Charente,	50	U10
Dalk. EH22		
Playfair Steps EH2	7	M16
The Mound		
Pleasance EH8	7	N16
Plewlands Av. EH10	31	K13
Plewlands Gdns. EH10	31	K13
Plewlands Ter. EH10	31	K13
Pleydell Pl. EH16	42	O12
Polton Dr., Lass. EH18	48	Q8
Polton Gdns., Lass. EH18	48	R8
Polton Rd., Lass. EH18	48	R8
Polton Rd., Loanh. EH20	48	P8
Polton St., Bonny. EH19	49	R8
Polton Ter., Lass. EH18	48	R8
Polwarth Cres. EH11	31	L15
Polwarth Gdns. EH11	31	K15
Polwarth Gro. EH11	31	K15
Polwarth Pk. EH11	31	K15
Polwarth Pl. EH11	31	K15
Polwarth Ter. EH11	31	K14
Ponton St. EH3	6	L15
Poplar La. EH6	12	O19
Porterfield Rd. EH4	10	K18
Portgower Pl. EH4	19	L17
Portland Pl. EH6	12	N19
North Junct. St.		
Portland St. EH6	12	N19
Portland Ter. EH6	12	N19
North Junct. St.		
Portobello High St. EH15	22	R17
Portobello Rd. EH8	22	P17
Portsburgh Sq. EH1	6	M16
West Port		
Potterrow EH8	7	M16
Pottery, The EH15	22	R17
Pipe La.		
Prestonfield Av. EH16	33	O14
Prestonfield Bk. EH16	33	O14
Prestonfield Cres. EH16	33	O14
Prestonfield Gdns. EH16	33	O14
Prestonfield Rd. EH16	33	O14
Prestonfield Ter. EH16	33	O14
Priestfield Av. EH16	33	O14
Priestfield Cres. EH16	33	O14
Priestfield Gdns. EH16	33	O14
Priestfield Gro. EH16	33	O15
Priestfield Rd. EH16	33	O15
Priestfield Rd. N. EH16	33	O15
Primrose Bk. Rd. EH5	11	L19
Primrose Cres., Dalk. EH22	50	V9
Primrose St. EH6	12	O18
Primrose Ter. EH11	30	K15
Primrose Ter., Dalk. EH22	50	V9
Prince Regent St. EH6	12	N19
Princes St. EH1	6	L16
Princes St. EH2	6	L16
Promenade EH15	22	Q18
Promenade, Muss. EH21	24	U16
Promenade Ter. EH15	22	R17
Prospect Bk. Cres. EH6	13	O18
Prospect Bk. Gdns. EH6	13	O18
Prospect Bk. Gro. EH6	13	P18
Prospect Bk. Pl. EH6	13	P18
Prospect Bk. Rd. EH6	13	O18
Prospect Bk. Ter. EH6	13	P18
Pryde Av., Bonny. EH19	49	R8
Pryde Ter., Bonny. EH19	48	R8
Quality St. EH4	9	G18
Quality St. La. EH4	9	G18
Quarry Clo. EH8	7	N15
Quarry Cotts. EH15	35	R14
Quarry Howe, Bal. EH14	45	C9
Deanpark Gro.		
Quarrybank EH14	38	F12
Quarrybank Clo. EH14	38	F12
Quarrybank Ct. EH14	38	F12
Quarrybank End EH14	38	F12
Quarryfoot Gdns., Bonny.	49	R8
EH19		
Quarryfoot Grn., Bonny. EH19	49	R8
Quarryfoot Gdns.		
Quarryfoot Pl., Bonny. EH19	49	R8
Quarryview EH14	38	F12
Quayside St. EH6	12	N19
Queen Charlotte La. EH6	12	O19
Queen Charlotte St.		
Queen Charlotte St. EH6	12	O19
Queen Margaret Clo. EH10	41	M11
Queen St. EH2	6	L17
Queen St. Gdns. E. EH3	6	M17
Queen St. Gdns. W. EH3	6	M17
Queen's Av. EH4	18	H17
Queen's Av. S. EH4	18	J17
Queen's Bay Cres. EH15	23	S16
Queen's Cres. EH9	32	N14
Queen's Dr. EH8	7	N16
Queen's Gdns. EH4	18	J17
Queen's Pk. Av. EH8	21	O17
Queen's Pk. Ct. EH8	21	P16
Queen's Rd. EH4	18	J17
Queen's Wk. EH16	34	Q14
Queensferry Rd. EH4	18	J17
Queensferry Rd.	8	E18
(Cram.) EH4		
Queensferry St. EH2	6	L16
Queensferry St. La. EH2	6	L16
Queensferry Ter. EH4	18	K17
Quilts, The EH6	12	N19
Quilts Wynd EH6	12	N19
Raeburn Ms. EH4	19	L17
Raeburn Pl. EH4	19	L17
Raeburn St. EH4	19	L17
Rae's Ct. EH16	42	O11
Rae's Gdns., Bonny. EH19	49	R8
Ramsay Gdn. EH1	6	M16
Ramsay La. EH1	6	M16
Ramsay Pl. EH15	22	R17
Randolph Cliff EH3	6	L16
Randolph Cres. EH3	6	L16
Randolph La. EH3	6	L16
Randolph Pl. EH3	6	L16
Rankeillor St. EH8	7	N15
Rankin Av. EH9	32	N13
Rankin Dr. EH9	32	N13
Rankin Rd. EH9	32	N14
Rannoch Gro. EH4	17	F17
Rannoch Pl. EH4	17	F17
Rannoch Rd. EH4	17	F17
Rannoch Ter. EH4	16	F17
Ransome Gdns. EH4	16	F17
Ratcliffe Ter. EH9	32	N14
Rathbone Pl. EH15	22	R17
Ratho Pk. Rd.	26	A13
(Ratho), Newbr. EH28		
Ravelrig Hill, Bal. EH14	44	B9
Ravelrig Pk., Bal. EH14	44	B9
Ravelrig Rd., Bal. EH14	44	B10
Ravelston Ct. EH12	18	J16
Ravelston Dykes EH4	18	J16
Ravelston Dykes EH12	18	J16
Ravelston Dykes La. EH4	18	H16
Ravelston Dykes Rd. EH4	18	H17
Ravelston Gdn. EH4	18	J16
Ravelston Heights EH4	18	H17
Ravelston Ho. Gro. EH4	18	J17
Ravelston Ho. Ln. EH4	18	J17
Ravelston Ho. Pk. EH4	18	J17
Ravelston Ho. Rd. EH4	18	J17
Ravelston Pk. EH4	18	K16
Ravelston Pl. EH4	19	K16
Belford Rd.		
Ravelston Ri. EH4	18	J16
Ravelston Ter. EH4	19	K17
Ravenscroft Gdns. EH17	43	Q11
Ravenscroft Pl. EH17	43	Q11
Ravenscroft St. EH17	43	Q11
Ravenswood Av. EH16	33	O13
Redbraes Gro. EH7	12	M18
Redbraes Pl. EH7	12	M18
Redcroft St., Dalk. EH22	51	R12
Redford EH13	40	J11
Redford Av. EH13	40	J11
Redford Bk. EH13	40	J11
Redford Cres. EH13	40	J11
Redford Dr. EH13	40	H11
Redford Gdns. EH13	40	J11
Redford Gro. EH13	40	J12
Redford Ln. EH13	40	J11
Redford Neuk EH13	40	J11
Redford Pl. EH13	40	J12
Redford Rd. EH13	40	J11
Redford Ter. EH13	40	J11
Redford Wk. EH13	40	J11
Redgauntlet Ter. EH16	33	P13
Redhall Av. EH14	29	H13
Redhall Bk. Rd. EH14	29	H13
Redhall Cres. EH14	29	H13
Redhall Dr. EH14	29	H13
Redhall Gdns. EH14	29	H13
Redhall Gro. EH14	29	H13
Redhall Ho. Dr. EH14	30	H13
Redhall Pl. EH14	29	H13
Redhall Rd. EH14	29	H13
Redhall Vw. EH14	30	H13
Redheughs Av. EH12	28	E14
Redheughs Rigg EH12	28	E15
Reekie's Ct. EH8	7	N16
Regent Bri. EH1	7	M17
Waterloo Pl.		
Regent Pl. EH7	21	O17
Regent Rd. EH1	7	N16
Regent Rd. EH7	7	N16
Regent St. EH15	23	R16
Regent St. La. EH15	23	R16
Regent Ter. EH7	7	N17
Regent Ter. Ms. EH7	7	N17
Regis Ct. EH4	8	E18
Register Pl. EH2	7	M17
Reid Ter. EH3	19	L17
Reid's Clo. EH8	7	N16
Reid's Ct. EH8	7	N16
Canongate		
Relugas Gdns. EH9	32	N14
Relugas Pl. EH9	32	N14
Relugas Rd. EH9	32	N14
Research Av. One	37	D12
(Ricc.), Currie EH14		
Research Av. Two	37	D12
(Ricc.), Currie EH14		
Research Pk. Rd.	37	D12
(Ricc.), Currie EH14		
Restalrig Av. EH7	21	P17
Restalrig Circ. EH7	13	P18
Restalrig Cres. EH7	13	P18
Restalrig Dr. EH7	21	P17
Restalrig Gdns. EH7	21	P17
Restalrig Pk. EH7	13	O18
Restalrig Rd. EH6	13	O18
Restalrig Rd. EH7	13	O18
Restalrig Rd. S. EH7	21	P17
Restalrig Sq. EH7	13	P18
Restalrig Ter. EH6	12	O18
Riccarton Av., Currie EH14	38	D11
Riccarton Cres., Currie EH14	38	D11
Riccarton Dr., Currie EH14	37	D11
Riccarton Gro., Currie EH14	38	E11
Riccarton Mains Rd., Currie	38	E11
EH14		
Richmond La. EH8	7	N16
Richmond Pl. EH8	7	N16
Richmond Ter. EH11	19	L16
Riding Pk. EH4	8	E18
Riego St. EH3	19	L16
Rillbank Cres. EH9	20	M15
Rillbank Ter. EH9	20	M15
Ringwood Pl. EH16	42	O12
Rintoul Pl. EH3	19	L17
Riselaw Cres. EH10	41	L12
Riselaw Pl. EH10	41	L12
Riselaw Rd. EH10	41	L12
Riselaw Ter. EH10	41	L12
Ritchie Pl. EH11	31	K15
Riversdale Cres. EH12	18	J15
Riversdale Gro. EH12	18	J16
Riversdale Rd. EH12	18	J16

Riverside Gdns., Muss. EH21	24	U15
Roanshead Rd.	50	V8
(Easth.), Dalk. EH22		
Robb's Ln. EH14	30	J14
Robb's Ln. Gro. EH14	30	J14
Robert Burns Dr.	33	O13
Robert Burn's Ms., Dalk. EH22	50	V10
Robertson Av. EH11	30	J15
Robertson's Clo. EH1	7	N16
Robertson's Clo., Dalk. EH22	50	U10
St. Andrew St.		
Robertson's Ct. EH8	7	N16
Calton Rd.		
Rocheid Pk. EH4	10	K18
Rocheid Path EH3	11	L18
Rochester Ter. EH10	31	L14
Rockville Ter., Bonny. EH19	49	R8
Roddinglaw EH12	26	C14
Roddinglaw Rd. EH12	26	C14
Rodney St. EH7	20	M17
Romero Pl. EH16	33	N15
Ronaldson's Wf. EH6	12	N19
Sandport Pl.		
Rose Pk. EH5	11	L19
Rose St. EH2	6	L16
Rose St. N. La. EH2	6	L16
Rose St. S. La. EH2	6	L16
Rosebank Cotts. EH3	6	L16
Rosebank Gdns. EH5	11	L19
Rosebank Gro. EH5	11	L19
Rosebank Rd. EH5	11	L19
Rosebery Cres. EH12	19	K16
Rosebery Cres. La. EH12	19	K16
Roseburn Av. EH12	18	J16
Roseburn Cliff EH12	18	J16
Roseburn Cres. EH12	18	J16
Roseburn Dr. EH12	18	J16
Roseburn Gdns. EH12	18	J16
Roseburn Pl. EH12	18	J16
Roseburn St. EH12	18	J15
Roseburn Ter. EH12	18	J16
Rosefield Av. EH15	22	R16
Rosefield Av. La. EH15	22	R16
Rosefield La. EH15	22	R16
Rosefield Pl. EH15	22	R16
Rosefield St. EH15	22	R16
Rosemount Bldgs. EH3	6	L16
Roseneath Pl. EH9	20	M15
Roseneath St. EH9	20	M15
Roseneath Ter. EH9	20	M15
Rosevale Pl. EH6	13	O18
Rosevale Ter. EH6	12	O18
Roseville Gdns. EH5	11	M19
Ross Gdns. EH9	32	N14
Ross Pl. EH9	32	N14
Ross Rd. EH16	33	O13
Rossie Pl. EH7	21	O17
Rosslyn Cres. EH6	12	N18
Rosslyn Ter. EH6	12	N18
Rothesay Ms. EH3	19	K16
Rothesay Pl. EH3	19	L16
Rothesay Pl., Muss. EH21	25	V15
Rothesay Ter. EH3	19	L16
Roull Gro. EH12	29	F15
Roull Pl. EH12	29	G15
Roull Rd. EH12	29	F15
Rowallan Ct. EH12	16	E16
Craigievar Wynd		
Rowan Tree Av., Currie EH14	45	D10
Rowan Tree Gro., Currie EH14	45	D10
Roxburgh Pl. EH8	7	N16
Roxburgh St. EH8	7	N16
Roxburgh Ter. EH8	7	N16
Drummond St.		
Royal Circ. EH3	6	L17
Royal Cres. EH3	20	M17
Royal Pk. Pl. EH8	21	O17
Royal Pk. Ter. EH8	21	O17
Royal Ter. EH7	7	N17
Royal Ter. Gdns. EH7	7	N17
Royal Ter. Ms. EH7	7	N17
Royston Mains Av. EH5	10	J19
Royston Mains Clo. EH5	10	K19
Royston Mains Cres. EH5	10	J19
Royston Mains Gdns. EH5	10	K19
Royston Mains Grn. EH5	10	K19
Royston Mains Pl. EH5	10	J19
Royston Mains Rd. EH5	10	K19
Royston Mains St. EH5	10	J19
Royston Ter. EH3	11	L18
Russell Pl. EH5	11	L19
Russell Rd. EH11	18	K15
Russell Rd. EH12	18	K16
Rustic Cotts. EH14	30	J13
Colinton Rd.		
Rutherford Dr. EH16	33	O13
Rutland Ct. EH3	6	L16
Rutland Ct. La. EH3	6	L16
Rutland Pl. EH1	6	L16
West End		
Rutland Sq. EH1	6	L16
Rutland St. EH1	6	L16
Ryehill Av. EH6	13	O18
Ryehill Gdns. EH6	13	O18
Ryehill Gro. EH6	13	O18
Ryehill Pl. EH6	13	O18
Ryehill Ter. EH6	13	O18
Saddletree Ln. EH16	33	P13
St. Alban's Rd. EH9	32	M14
St. Andrew Pl. EH6	12	O18
St. Andrew Sq. EH1	7	M17
St. Andrew Sq. EH2	7	M17
St. Andrew St., Dalk. EH22	50	U10
St. Anthony Ct. EH6	12	N19
St. Anthony St.		
St. Anthony La. EH6	12	N19
St. Anthony St.		
St. Anthony Pl. EH6	12	N19
St. Anthony St. EH6	12	N19
St. Bernard's Cres. EH4	6	L17
St. Bernard's Pl. EH3	19	L17
Saunders St.		
St. Bernard's Row EH4	19	L17
St. Catherine's Gdns. EH12	17	H15
St. Catherine's Pl. EH9	32	N15
St. Clair Av. EH6	12	O18
St. Clair Pl. EH6	12	O18
St. Clair Rd. EH6	12	O18
St. Clair St. EH6	12	O18
St. Clair Ter. EH10	31	K13
St. Colme St. EH3	6	L16
St. David's Pl. EH3	6	L16
Morrison St.		
St. David's Ter. EH3	6	L16
Morrison St.		
St. Fillan's Ter. EH10	31	L13
St. Giles' St. EH1	7	M16
St. James Cen. EH1	7	M17
St. James Pl. EH1	7	M17
St. James Sq. EH1	7	M17
James Craig Wk.		
St. John St. EH8	7	N16
St. John's Av. EH12	17	G15
St. John's Cres. EH12	17	G15
St. John's Gdns. EH12	17	G15
St. John's Hill EH8	7	N16
St. John's Pl. EH8	7	N16
Holyrood Rd.		
St. John's Rd. EH12	16	F15
St. John's Ter. EH12	17	G15
St. Katharine's Brae EH16	42	O11
St. Katharine's Cres. EH16	42	O11
St. Katharine's Ln. EH16	42	O11
St. Leonard's Bk. EH8	7	N15
St. Leonard's Crag EH8	7	N15
St. Leonard's Hill EH8	7	N15
St. Leonard's La. EH8	7	N15
St. Leonard's St. EH8	20	N15
St. Margaret's Pl. EH9	32	M14
St. Margaret's Rd. EH9	31	L14
St. Mark's La. EH15	23	R16
St. Mark's Pl. EH15	23	R16
St. Mary's Pl. EH15	23	S16
St. Mary's Pl. La. EH15	23	S16
St. Mary's St. EH1	7	N16
St. Michael's Av., Muss. EH21	25	V15
St. Ninian's Dr. EH12	16	F16
St. Ninian's Rd. EH12	16	F16
St. Ninian's Ter. EH10	31	K13
St. Patrick Sq. EH8	7	N15
St. Patrick St. EH8	7	N15
St. Peter's Bldgs. EH3	19	L15
Gilmore Pl.		
St. Peter's Pl. EH3	19	L15
St. Ronan's Ter. EH10	31	L13
St. Stephen Pl. EH3	19	L17
St. Stephen St.		
St. Stephen St. EH3	6	L17
St. Teresa Pl. EH10	31	L14
St. Thomas Rd. EH9	32	M14
St. Vincent St. EH3	6	L17
Salamander Pl. EH6	12	O19
Salamander St. EH6	12	O19
Salisbury Pl. EH9	32	N15
Salisbury Rd. EH16	32	N15
Salmond Pl. EH7	21	O17
Salter's Gro., Dalk. EH22	50	V10
Salter's Rd., Dalk. EH22	50	V10
Salter's Rd., Muss. EH21	25	W13
Salter's Ter., Dalk. EH22	50	V10
Saltire Society EH1	7	M16
High St.		
Salvesen Cres. EH4	9	H19
Salvesen Gdns. EH4	9	H19
Salvesen Gro. EH4	9	H19
Salvesen Ter. EH4	9	H19
Sandford Gdns. EH15	22	R16
Sandport EH6	12	O19
Sandport Gdns. EH6	12	N19
Sandport Pl. EH6	12	N19
Sandport St. EH6	12	N19
Sauchiebank EH11	18	K15
Saughton Av. EH11	30	J15
Saughton Cres. EH12	18	H15
Saughton Gdns. EH12	18	H15
Saughton Gro. EH12	18	H15
Saughton Ln. EH12	18	H15
Saughton Mains Av. EH11	29	G14
Saughton Mains Bk. EH11	29	H14
Saughton Mains Cotts. EH11	29	G14
Saughton Mains Gdns.		
Saughton Mains Dr. EH11	29	G14
Saughton Mains Gdns. EH11	29	G14
Saughton Mains Gro. EH11	29	H14
Saughton Mains Ln. EH11	29	G14
Saughton Mains Pk. EH11	29	G14
Saughton Mains Pl. EH11	29	G14
Saughton Mains St. EH11	29	G14
Saughton Mains Ter. EH11	29	G14
Saughton Pk. EH12	18	H15
Saughton Rd. EH11	29	G14
Saughton Rd. N. EH12	29	G15
Saughtonhall Av. EH12	18	H15
Saughtonhall Av. W. EH12	18	H15
Saughtonhall Circ. EH12	18	J15
Saughtonhall Cres. EH12	18	H15
Saughtonhall Dr. EH12	18	H15
Saughtonhall Gdns. EH12	18	J15
Saughtonhall Gro. EH12	18	J15
Saughtonhall Pl. EH12	18	H15
Saughtonhall Ter. EH12	18	J15
Saunders St. EH3	6	L17
Savile Pl. EH9	32	N14
Savile Ter. EH9	32	N14
Saxe Coburg St. EH3	19	L17
Saxe-Coburg Pl. EH3	19	L17
Saxe-Coburg Ter. EH3	19	L17
Saxe Coburg St.		
School Brae EH4	8	E19
School Brae, Lass. EH18	48	R9
School Grn., Lass. EH18	49	R9
Sciennes EH9	32	N15
Sciennes Gdns. EH9	32	N15
Sciennes Hill Pl. EH9	32	N15
Sciennes		
Sciennes Ho. Dr. EH9	32	N15
Sciennes		
Sciennes Ho. Pl. EH9	32	N15
Sciennes Pl. EH9	32	N15
Sciennes Rd. EH9	32	M15
Scollon Av., Bonny. EH19	49	S8
Scone Gdns. EH8	21	P17
Scotland St. EH3	20	M17
Seacot EH6	13	P18
Seafield Av. EH6	13	P18
Seafield Moor Rd. EH10	46	M9
Seafield Pl. EH6	13	P18
Seafield Rd. EH6	13	P18
Seafield Rd. E. EH6	22	Q16
Seafield St. EH6	13	P18
Seafield Ter. EH6	13	P18
Seafield Av.		
Seafield Way EH15	13	Q18
Seaforth Dr. EH4	18	J17
Seaforth Ter. EH4	18	J17
Sealcarr St. EH5	10	K20
Seaport St. EH6	12	O19
Bernard St.		
Seaview Cres. EH15	23	S16
Seaview Ter. EH15	23	S16
Second Gait	37	D12
(Ricc.), Currie EH14		
Semple St. EH3	6	*L16

Name	Pg	Ref
Seton Pl. EH9	32	N15
Shadepark Cres., Dalk. EH22	50	U10
Shadepark Dr., Dalk. EH22	50	U10
Shadepark Gdns., Dalk. EH22	50	U10
Shaftesbury Pk. EH11	30	K14
Shandon Cres. EH11	30	K14
Shandon Pl. EH11	30	K14
Shandon Rd. EH11	30	K14
Shandon St. EH11	30	K14
Shandon Ter. EH11	30	K14
Shandwick Pl. EH2	6	L16
Shanter Way EH16	33	O13
Cumnor Cres.		
Sharpdale Ln. EH16	33	O13
Shaw's Pl. EH7	12	N18
Shaw's Sq. EH1	20	N17
Gayfield Sq.		
Shaw's St. EH7	12	N18
Shaw's Ter. EH7	12	N18
Sheriff Bk. EH6	12	N19
Sheriff Brae EH6	12	N19
Sheriff Pk. EH6	12	N19
Shore EH6	12	O19
Shore Pl. EH6	12	O19
Shorthope St., Muss. EH21	25	V15
Shrub Mt. EH15	22	R17
Shrub Pl. EH7	12	N18
Shrub Pl. La. EH7	20	N17
Shrub Pl.		
Sienna Gdns. EH9	32	N15
Sighthill Av. EH11	29	G13
Sighthill Bk. EH11	28	F13
Sighthill Ct. EH11	28	F13
Sighthill Cres. EH11	28	F13
Sighthill Dr. EH11	28	F13
Sighthill Gdns. EH11	29	F13
Sighthill Grn. EH11	28	F13
Sighthill Gro. EH11	29	G13
Sighthill Ln. EH11	28	F13
Sighthill Neuk EH11	28	F13
Sighthill Pk. EH11	29	F13
Sighthill Pl. EH11	28	F13
Sighthill Ri. EH11	28	F13
Sighthill Rd. EH11	28	F13
Sighthill St. EH11	28	F13
Sighthill Ter. EH11	29	F13
Sighthill Vw. EH11	28	F13
Sighthill Wynd EH11	28	F13
Silverknowes Av. EH4	9	G18
Silverknowes Bk. EH4	9	G18
Silverknowes Brae EH4	9	G18
Silverknowes Ct. EH4	9	G18
Silverknowes Cres. EH4	9	G18
Silverknowes Dell EH4	9	G18
Silverknowes Dr. EH4	9	G18
Silverknowes Eastway EH4	9	G18
Silverknowes Gdns. EH4	9	G19
Silverknowes Grn. EH4	9	H18
Silverknowes Gro. EH4	9	G19
Silverknowes Hill EH4	9	G18
Silverknowes Ln. EH4	9	G18
Silverknowes Midway EH4	9	H18
Silverknowes Neuk EH4	9	H18
Silverknowes Parkway EH4	9	G19
Silverknowes Pl. EH4	9	G19
Silverknowes Rd. EH4	9	G19
Silverknowes Rd. E. EH4	9	G18
Silverknowes Rd. S. EH4	9	G18
Silverknowes Southway EH4	9	H18
Silverknowes Ter. EH4	9	G18
Silverknowes Vw. EH4	9	H18
Silvermills EH3	19	L17
Simon Sq. EH8	7	N16
Sir Harry Lauder Rd. EH15	22	R16
Slaeside, Bal. EH14	45	C9
Slateford Rd. EH11	30	J14
Slateford Rd. EH14	30	J14
Sleigh Dr. EH7	21	O17
Sleigh Gdns. EH7	21	P17
Sloan St. EH6	12	N18
Smeaton Gro.		
(Inver.), Muss. EH21	25	V14
Smithfield St. EH11	30	J15
Smith's Pl. EH6	12	N18
Smithy Grn. Av.	51	R12
(Dand.), Dalk. EH22		
Society EH1	7	M16
Chambers St.		
Solicitor's Bldgs. EH1	7	M16
Cowgate		
Somerset Pl. EH6	12	O18
Sour Howe EH13	40	K11
South Barnton Av. EH4	9	G18
South Beechwood EH12	17	H15
South Bri. EH1	7	M16
South Bri. EH8	7	M16
South Charlotte St. EH2	6	L16
South Clerk St. EH8	20	N15
South Coll. St. EH8	7	M16
South E. Circ. Pl. EH3	6	L17
South Elixa Pl. EH8	22	P16
South Ettrick Rd. EH10	31	K14
South Fort St. EH6	12	N19
South Gayfield La. EH1	20	N17
Gayfield Sq.		
South Gillsland Rd. EH10	31	K14
South Gray St. EH9	32	N14
South Gray's Clo. EH1	7	N16
South Groathill Av. EH4	18	J17
South Gyle Access EH12	28	F14
South Gyle Bdy. EH12	27	D15
South Gyle Cres. EH12	28	E14
South Gyle Cres. La. EH12	28	E14
South Gyle Gdns. EH12	28	E15
South Gyle Ln. EH12	28	E15
South Gyle Mains EH12	28	E15
South Gyle Pk. EH12	28	E15
South Gyle Rd. EH12	28	E15
South Gyle Wynd EH12	28	F14
South Lauder Rd. EH9	32	N14
South Laverockbank Av. EH5	11	M19
South Learmonth Av. EH4	19	K17
South Learmonth Gdns. EH4	19	K17
South Lorne Pl. EH6	12	N18
South Maybury EH12	16	E15
South Meadow Wk. EH9	32	M15
Roseneath Ter.		
South Mellis Pk. EH8	22	Q16
South Morton St. EH15	23	S16
South Oswald Rd. EH9	32	M14
South Oxford St. EH8	32	N15
South Pk. EH6	11	M19
South St. Andrew St. EH2	7	M17
South St. David St. EH2	7	M17
South Sloan St. EH6	12	N18
South Steil EH10	30	K13
South St., Dalk. EH22	50	U10
South St., Muss. EH21	24	U15
South Trinity Rd. EH5	11	L19
Southfield Bk. EH15	22	Q15
Southfield Fm. Gro. EH15	22	Q16
Southfield Gdns. E. EH15	22	Q16
Southfield Gdns. W. EH15	22	Q16
Southfield Ln. EH15	22	Q15
Southfield Pl. EH15	22	R16
Southfield Pl. N. EH15	22	Q15
Southfield Sq.		
Southfield Pl. S. EH15	22	Q15
Southfield Sq.		
Southfield Rd. E. EH15	22	Q15
Southfield Rd. W. EH15	22	Q15
Southfield Sq. EH15	22	Q15
Southfield Ter. EH15	22	Q15
Southfield Vills. EH15	22	R16
Stanley La.		
Southhouse Av. EH17	42	O11
Southhouse Bdy. EH17	42	O10
Southhouse Cres. EH17	43	O10
Southhouse Gdns. EH17	42	O10
Southhouse Gro. EH17	42	O10
Southhouse Ln. EH17	42	O11
Southhouse Medway EH17	43	O11
Southhouse Path EH17	43	O11
Southhouse Rd. EH17	42	O11
Southhouse Sq. EH17	43	O10
Southhouse Ter. EH17	43	P11
Soutra Ct. EH16	43	O11
Spa Pl. EH15	22	R17
Spalding Cres., Dalk. EH22	50	U10
Speedwell Av., Dalk. EH22	51	R12
Spence St. EH16	33	N15
Spencer Pl. EH5	11	L19
Spey St. EH7	12	N18
Spey St. La. EH7	12	N18
Spey Ter. EH7	12	N18
Spiers Pl. EH6	12	N19
Spinney, The EH17	43	P11
Spittal St. EH3	6	L16
Spittal St. La. EH3	6	L16
Spittalfield Cres. EH8	20	N15
St. Leonard's St.		
Spottiswoode Rd. EH9	32	M15
Spottiswoode St. EH9	32	M15
Spring Gdns. EH8	21	O17
Springfield EH6	12	N18
Springfield Bldgs. EH6	12	N18
Springfield St.		
Springfield La. EH6	12	N18
Springfield St. EH6	12	N18
Springvalley Gdns. EH10	31	L14
Springvalley Ter. EH10	31	L14
Springwell Pl. EH11	19	K15
Springwood Pk. EH16	42	O12
Spylaw Av. EH13	39	G12
Spylaw Bk. Rd. EH13	39	G12
Spylaw Ho. EH13	39	H11
Spylaw Pk. EH13	39	G12
Spylaw Rd. EH10	31	K14
Spylaw St. EH13	39	H11
Square, The	51	R12
(Dand.), Dalk. EH22		
Stable La. EH10	31	L14
Stafford St. EH3	6	L16
Stair Pk. EH12	18	J16
Stanedykehead EH16	42	N11
Stanhope Pl. EH12	19	K16
Stanhope St. EH12	19	K16
Stanley Pl. EH7	21	O17
Stanley Rd. EH6	11	M19
Stanley St. EH15	22	R16
Stanwell St. EH6	12	N18
Stapeley Av. EH7	22	Q17
Starbank Rd. EH5	11	M19
Station Brae EH15	22	R16
Station Ln., Bal. EH14	45	C10
Station Rd. EH12	17	G15
Station Rd., Dalk. EH22	50	T9
Station Rd., Loanh. EH20	48	P8
Station Rd., Muss. EH21	24	U15
Stead's Pl. EH6	12	N18
Steel's Pl. EH10	31	L14
Steils, The EH10	40	K12
Stenhouse Av. EH11	29	H14
Stenhouse Av. W. EH11	29	H14
Stenhouse Cotts. EH11	29	H14
Stenhouse Cres. EH11	29	H14
Stenhouse Cross EH11	29	H14
Stenhouse Dr. EH11	29	H14
Stenhouse Gdns. EH11	29	H14
Stenhouse Gdns. N. EH11	29	H14
Stenhouse Gro. EH11	29	H14
Stenhouse Mill Cres. EH11	29	H14
Stenhouse Mill La. EH11	29	H14
Stenhouse Mill Wynd EH11	29	H14
Stenhouse Pl. E. EH11	29	H14
Stenhouse Pl. W. EH11	29	H14
Stenhouse Rd. EH11	29	H14
Stenhouse St. E. EH11	29	H14
Stenhouse St. W. EH11	29	G14
Stenhouse Ter. EH11	29	H14
Stennis Gdns. EH17	43	P12
Stevenlaw's Clo. EH1	7	M16
High St.		
Stevenson Av. EH11	30	J15
Stevenson Dr. EH11	29	H14
Stevenson Gro. EH11	30	J15
Stevenson Rd. EH11	30	J15
Stevenson Ter. EH11	30	J15
Stewart Av., Currie EH14	37	D10
Stewart Cres., Currie EH14	37	D10
Stewart Gdns., Currie EH14	37	D10
Stewart Gro., Dalk. EH22	51	R12
Stewart Pl., Currie EH14	37	D10
Stewart Rd., Currie EH14	37	D10
Stewart Ter. EH11	30	J15
Stewartfield EH6	12	M18
Stirling Rd. EH5	11	L19
Stoneybank Av., Muss. EH21	24	U14
Stoneybank Ct., Muss. EH21	24	U15
Stoneybank Cres., Muss. EH21	24	U14
Stoneybank Dr., Muss. EH21	24	U15
Stoneybank Gdns.,	24	U15
Muss. EH21		
Stoneybank Gdns. N.,	24	U15
Muss. EH21		
Stoneybank Gdns. S.,	24	U14
Muss. EH21		
Stoneybank Gro.,	24	U14
Muss. EH21		
Stoneybank Pl., Muss. EH21	24	U14
Stoneybank Rd., Muss. EH21	24	U14
Stoneybank Ter., Muss. EH21	24	U14
Stoneyhill Av., Muss. EH21	24	U15

Street	Page	Grid
Wardie Rd. EH5	11	L19
Wardie Sq. EH5	11	L19
Wardie Steps EH5	11	L19
Wardieburn Dr. EH5	11	K19
Wardieburn Pl. E. EH5	10	K19
Wardieburn Pl. N. EH5	10	K19
Wardieburn Pl. S. EH5	10	K19
Wardieburn Pl. W. EH5	10	K19
Wardieburn Rd. EH5	10	K19
Wardieburn St. E. EH5	10	K19
Wardieburn St. W. EH5	10	K19
Wardieburn Ter. EH5	10	K19
Wardiefield EH5	11	K19
Wardlaw Pl. EH11	30	K15
Wardlaw St. EH11	30	K15
Wardlaw Ter. EH11	30	K15
Warrender Pk. Cres. EH9	31	L15
Warrender Pk. Rd. EH9	32	M15
Warrender Pk. Ter. EH9	32	M15
Warriston Av. EH3	11	M18
Warriston Clo. EH1	7	M16
High St.		
Warriston Cres. EH3	11	M18
Warriston Dr. EH3	11	L18
Warriston Gdns. EH3	11	L18
Warriston Gro. EH3	11	L18
Warriston Pl. EH3	11	M18
Warriston Rd. EH3	11	M19
Warriston Rd. EH7	11	M19
Warriston Ter. EH3	11	L18
Washington La. EH11	19	K15
Washington St. EH11	19	K15
Water St. EH6	12	O19
Waterfall Wk., Dalk. EH22	50	U9
Bruce Gdns.		
Waterloo Pl. EH1	7	M17
Water's Clo. EH6	12	O19
Shore		
Waterside Ct. EH12	18	J16
Coltbridge Av.		
Watertoun Rd. EH9	32	N14
Watson Cres. EH11	31	K15
Watson's Bldgs. EH4	9	G18
Main St.		
Watts Clo., Muss. EH21	24	U15
Wauchope Av. EH16	34	Q14
Wauchope Cres. EH16	34	Q14
Wauchope Ho. EH16	34	Q14
Wauchope Pl. EH16	34	Q14
Wauchope Rd. EH16	34	Q14
Wauchope Sq. EH16	34	Q14
Wauchope Ter. EH16	34	Q14
Waugh Path, Bonny. EH19	49	S8
Waulkmill Ln., Currie EH14	45	D10
Waverley Bri. EH1	7	M16
Waverley Ct., Bonny. EH19	49	S8
Waverley Cres., Bonny. EH19	49	S8
Waverley Dr., Bonny. EH19	49	S8
Waverley Pk. EH8	21	O17
Waverley Pk., Bonny. EH19	49	S8
Waverley Pk. Ter. EH8	21	O17
Waverley Pl. EH7	21	O17
Waverley Rd., Bonny. EH19	49	S8
Waverley Rd., Dalk. EH22	50	T9
Waverley Steps EH2	7	M16
Waverley Ter., Bonny. EH19	49	S8
Weaver's Knowe Cres., Currie EH14	37	D11
Websters Land EH1	6	M16
West Port		
Wedderburn Ter.	25	V14
(Inver.), Muss. EH21		
Wee Brae, Lass. EH18	49	R9
Weir Ct. EH11	29	F13
Weir Cres., Dalk. EH22	50	T9
Well Ct. EH4	19	L16
Wellington Pl. EH6	12	O19
Wellington St. EH7	7	N17
Wemyss Pl. EH3	6	L17
Wemyss Pl. Ms. EH3	6	L17
West Adam St. EH8	7	N16
West Annandale St. EH7	12	M18
West App. Rd. EH3	6	L15
West App. Rd. EH11	6	L15
West Bow EH1	6	M16
West Bowling Grn. St. EH6	12	N19
West Brighton Cres. EH15	22	R16
West Bryson Rd. EH11	31	K15
West Caiystane Rd. EH10	41	L11
West Carnethy Av. EH13	39	H11
West Castle Rd. EH10	31	L15
West Catherine Pl. EH12	18	K16
West Coates EH12	18	K16
West Coll. St. EH8	7	M16
West Ct. EH4	18	J17
West Ct. EH16	34	Q14
West Craigs Av. EH12	15	D15
West Craigs Cres. EH12	15	D15
West Craigs Ind. Est. EH12	15	D16
West Cft.	26	A13
(Ratho), Newbr. EH28		
West Cromwell St. EH6	12	N19
Cromwell Pl.		
West Crosscauseway EH8	7	N15
West End EH2	6	L16
West End Pl. EH11	19	K15
West Ferryfield EH5	11	K18
West Fountain Pl. EH11	19	K15
West Gorgie Parks EH14	30	J14
West Gra. Gdns. EH9	32	M14
Grange Ln.		
West Granton Grn. EH4	10	H19
West Granton Gro. EH4	10	J19
West Granton Rd. EH5	10	J19
West Harbour Rd. EH5	10	K20
West Holmes Gdns.,	24	U15
Muss. EH21		
West Mains Rd. EH9	32	N13
West Maitland St. EH12	19	L16
West Mayfield EH9	32	N14
West Mill Ct., Lass. EH18	49	R8
Westmill Rd.		
West Mill La. EH4	19	K17
Dean Path		
West Mill Rd. EH13	39	G11
West Montgomery Pl. EH7	20	N17
West Newington Pl. EH9	32	N15
West Nicolson St. EH8	7	N16
West Norton Pl. EH7	20	N17
West Pk. Pl. EH11	19	K15
West Pier EH5	10	K20
West Pilton Av. EH4	10	J18
West Pilton Bk. EH4	10	H19
West Pilton Cres. EH4	10	H19
West Pilton Crossway EH4	10	J19
West Pilton Dr. EH4	10	J19
West Pilton Gdns. EH4	10	J19
West Pilton Grn. EH4	10	J19
West Pilton Gro. EH4	10	J19
West Pilton Lea EH4	10	J19
West Pilton Ln. EH4	10	J19
West Pilton March EH4	10	J19
West Pilton Pk. EH4	10	J19
West Pilton Pl. EH4	10	J19
West Pilton Ri. EH4	10	J19
West Pilton Rd. EH4	10	J19
West Pilton St. EH4	10	J19
West Pilton Ter. EH4	10	J19
West Pilton Vw. EH4	10	J18
West Port EH1	6	M16
West Port EH3	6	M16
West Powburn EH9	32	N14
West Preston St. EH8	32	N15
West Register St. EH2	7	M17
West Relugas Rd. EH9	32	M14
West Richmond St. EH8	7	N16
West Savile Rd. EH16	32	N14
West Savile Ter. EH9	32	N14
West Scotland St. La. EH3	20	M17
West Shore Rd. EH5	10	H19
West Silvermills La. EH3	19	L17
West Stanhope Pl. EH12	19	K16
Stanhope Pl.		
West Telferton EH7	22	Q17
West Tollcross EH3	6	L15
West Werberside EH4	10	K18
West Winnelstrae EH5	10	K18
West Wds. EH4	10	K18
Westbank Ln. EH15	22	R17
Westbank Pl. EH15	22	R17
Westbank St. EH15	22	R17
Westburn Av. EH14	38	F12
Westburn Gdns. EH14	38	F12
Westburn Gro. EH14	38	F12
Westburn Middlefield EH14	38	F12
Westburn Pk. EH14	38	F12
Wester Broom Av. EH12	28	F15
Wester Broom Dr. EH12	28	F15
Wester Broom Gdns. EH12	28	F15
Wester Broom Gro. EH12	28	F15
Wester Broom Pl. EH12	28	F15
Wester Broom Ter. EH12	28	F15
Wester Clo. EH6	11	M20
Newhaven Main St.		
Wester Coates Av. EH12	18	K16
Wester Coates Gdns. EH12	18	K16
Wester Coates Pl. EH12	19	K16
Wester Coates Rd. EH12	18	K16
Wester Coates Ter. EH12	18	K16
Wester Drylaw Av. EH4	10	H18
Wester Drylaw Dr. EH4	10	H18
Wester Drylaw Pk. EH4	10	J18
Wester Drylaw Pl. EH4	10	H18
Wester Drylaw Row EH4	18	J17
Wester Hailes Cen. EH14	38	F12
Wester Hailes Dr. EH14	38	F12
Wester Hailes Pk. EH14	39	G12
Wester Hailes Rd. EH14	28	F13
Wester Hailes Rd. EH14	28	F13
Wester Hailes Rd.,	28	F13
Jun.Grn. EH14		
Wester Hill EH10	40	K12
Wester Row, Currie EH14	27	D13
Wester Steil EH10	30	K13
Western Cor. EH12	18	H16
Saughtonhall Dr.		
Western Gdns. EH12	18	J16
Western Harbour EH6	12	N20
Western Pl. EH12	18	J16
Western Ter. EH12	18	J16
Westfield Av. EH11	30	J15
Westfield Ct. EH11	30	J15
Westfield Ct., Dalk. EH22	50	T9
Westfield Dr., Dalk. EH22	50	T9
Westfield Gro., Dalk. EH22	50	T9
Westfield Pk., Dalk. EH22	50	T9
Westfield Rd. EH11	30	J15
Westfield St. EH11	30	J15
Westgarth Av. EH13	39	H11
Westhall Gdns. EH10	31	L15
Westland Cotts. EH17	43	Q11
Ravenscroft Pl.		
Westland Hos. EH17	43	Q11
Ravenscroft Pl.		
Westmill Rd., Lass. EH18	49	R8
Westmill Wynd, Lass. EH18	49	R8
Westmost Clo. EH6	11	M20
Newhaven Main St.		
Westside Plaza EH14	38	F12
Murrayburn Gate		
Wheatfield Gro., Loanh. EH20	47	O8
Wheatfield Ln., Loanh. EH20	47	O9
Wheatfield Pl. EH11	30	J15
Wheatfield Rd. EH11	30	J15
Wheatfield St. EH11	30	K15
Wheatfield Ter. EH11	30	J15
Wheatfield Wk., Loanh. EH20	47	O8
Wheatsheaf La., Dalk. EH22	50	U10
Whins Pl. EH15	22	R17
Figgate St.		
White Dales EH10	41	M11
White Hart St., Dalk. EH22	50	U10
Buccleuch St.		
White Horse Clo. EH8	7	N16
White Pk. EH11	30	K15
Whitehall Ct. EH4	18	H17
Whitehill Av., Muss. EH21	24	U15
Whitehill Dr., Dalk. EH22	50	V9
Whitehill Fm. Rd.,	24	U14
Muss. EH21		
Whitehill Gdns., Muss. EH21	24	U14
Whitehill Gro., Dalk. EH22	50	V9
Whitehill Rd. EH15	35	S14
Whitehill Rd., Dalk. EH22	35	S14
Whitehill Rd.	35	S14
(Newcr.), Muss. EH21		
Whitehill St.	35	S14
(Newcr.), Muss. EH21		
Whitehouse Ln. EH9	31	L15
Whitehouse Rd. EH4	8	E18
Whitehouse Ter. EH9	32	M14
Whitelea Cres., Bal. EH14	44	C8
Whitelea Rd., Bal. EH14	44	B8
Whites Clo., Dalk. EH22	50	U10
St. Andrew St.		
Whitingford EH6	12	M19
Whitson Cres. EH11	30	H15
Whitson Gro. EH11	30	H15
Whitson Pl. E. EH11	30	H15
Whitson Pl. W. EH11	30	H15
Whitson Rd. EH11	30	H15
Whitson Ter. EH11	30	H15
Whitson Wk. EH11	30	H15

INDEX TO PLACES OF INTEREST